B Rhodes

Three Apostles of Quakerism

Popular Sketches of Fox, Penn and Barclay

B Rhodes

Three Apostles of Quakerism
Popular Sketches of Fox, Penn and Barclay

ISBN/EAN: 9783337404420

Printed in Europe, USA, Canada, Australia, Japan

Cover: Foto ©Lupo / pixelio.de

More available books at **www.hansebooks.com**

THREE APOSTLES OF QUAKERISM,

POPULAR SKETCHES OF

FOX, PENN AND BARCLAY,

By B. RHODES,

Author of "John Bright, Statesman and Orator," &c.

With Introduction by J. STOUGHTON, D.D.,
Author of "Ecclesiastical History of England,"
"Life of William Penn," &c., &c.

"They pleaded only for broad, unfettered, spiritual Christianity."—
J. J. Gurney. *Memoirs*, vol. ii, p. 27.

INTRODUCTION.

I HAVE been requested by the Author of this Volume to write a few introductory lines; with that request I cheerfully comply. Having read the proof sheets, I can testify to the diligence, care, and ability, with which the work has been executed. The perusal has been to me very interesting and very pleasant; and I have felt much satisfaction at finding that the historical conclusions here presented are, in general, coincident with my own.

It might be supposed that a book of this limited size, and intended for popular circulation, would be based chiefly, if not entirely, on the larger and best known biographies and histories relative to the men and the period described. But this is by no means the case. I find in these pages numerous signs of original research, and abundant evidence that the writer has formed an independent judgment of the questions coming before him in his enquiries. He has had access to some unpublished correspondence, of which he has made good use. Fourteen letters, not printed before, are laid under contribution, and they add much to the value of the volume.

Mr. Rhodes has evidently much sympathy with the life and labours of the early Quakers; and not being a member of that Society, he is free to judge impartially of certain points in their singular history. That judgment he has wisely exercised. I am fully persuaded in my own mind that Quakerism was a salutary reaction against the formalities, and the hard theological systematising of the age; that it called attention to forgotten truths; and that its excitements, though clouded by some smoke, yet burnt with fire from heaven; also I quite concur with the writer in thinking that the Society of Friends have still a place for good amongst religious agencies at work in this nineteenth century. May they have grace successfully to accomplish their mission!

I may add, that whilst all three of these biographical sketches are valuable contributions to our ecclesiastical literature, the last, which treats of Robert Barclay, is the fullest, most original, and best of all.

JOHN STOUGHTON.

PREFACE.

The demand of this busy age is for small books, containing the pith and marrow of important subjects. As regards my subject, I have endeavoured to meet this demand. I hope that the volume supplies at once sketches of three leaders in early Quaker history, and an informal manual of the rise and tenets of the Society.

A few years ago, I was led to re-examine the journal of George Fox, and I was surprised to find him an evangelist of a rare order, with a heart burning and throbbing with pity for sinners and with zeal for the Master. His ardent nature was laid hold of by the gospel in its fulness, and the result was a spirituality at once delicate and strong.

The same features attracted me in William Penn. He also had many of the gifts of the evangelist. He could collect and hold a crowd almost as well as Fox, and preach them as full a gospel. If other schemes had not claimed so large a share of his life, I think he might have done an evangelistic work equal to that done by George Fox.

Robert Barclay deserves to be highly honoured as one who truly devoted his all to Christ. And he had much to devote—an honoured name and titled connections, rare intellectual gifts and great acquirements, social position and wealth. Yet if I understand his life aright, there was no half-heartedness in his decision. But I miss in him that glowing and vigorous assertion of gospel truths which delights us in the pages of Fox and Penn. The pungent and arousing appeals which stud like gems the writings of his two brethren are not to be found in his pages. Silent waiting on God is urged, entire self-surrender to God on the part of the Christian is insisted on with great earnestness. But the reader will look in vain, even in passages which seem to invite them, for earnest calls to repentance or to diligent service of the gospel of Christ.

The Quakerism of the eighteenth century followed Barclay. The work of Fox was dropped. No one continued his vigorous aggression, but repression of activity was advocated openly. To this I venture to trace the decline of the Society in those days. In the Quakerism of to-day, I think I see Fox's spirit, and I would fain help the healthy reaction, however feebly, by these sketches. I hope they will also introduce to some Christians of other denominations three beautiful examples of spiritual-mindedness.

In the preparation of the sketches of Penn and Barclay, I have had access to numerous unpublished letters in the keeping of a member of the Barclay family. For these I desire to express my warmest thanks. I have used them sparingly. A list of those from which I give extracts will be found on the next page. To the best of my knowledge these extracts have not been printed before.

It is not probable that I shall continue the series of sketches to which this trio forms an appropriate introduction. But I am glad thus to acknowledge my indebtedness to a Society to which I owe more than I can ever repay. None of its members long more fervently than I do that the spirit and labours of its first days may distinguish it again.

Batheaston,
    near Bath.

LIST OF LETTERS

(HITHERTO UNPUBLISHED).

From which extracts are given in this volume.

From Geo. Fox to Robert Barclay, dated 16. x. 1675, quoted pp. 84, 113
" Geo. Keith to R. Barclay, 12. III. 1676.......................... 54, 114
" D. Barclay to R. Barclay   do. 113
" R. Barclay to the Princess Elizabeth, 6. VII. 1676................. 121
" the Princess Elizabeth to R. Barclay, Dec. 1. 1676............... 122
         Do.   do.   Mar. 1. 1677............... 126
         Do.   do.   July 6. 1677............... 126
" R. Barclay to the Princess Elizabeth, 6. v. 1679.................... 127
" the Duke of York to R. Barclay, June 27th, 1680................ 131
" Geo. Fox to R. Barclay, 31. IV. 1680................................... 129
" Christian Barclay to Friends in Aberdeen, 15. VI. 1693.......... 95
" Wm. Penn to R. Barclay, junr., 7. XII. 1694......................... 71
" Hy. Gouldney to R. Barclay, junr., 28. XII. 1694.................. 70
" Sir D. Dalrymple to R. Barclay, junr., July 4th, 1710............ 76

R. Barclay's "Vindication" quoted pp. 91, 120, 137, 138.

GEORGE FOX,

THE

FIRST OF THE QUAKERS.

"This man, the first of the Quakers, and by trade a Shoemaker, was one of those to whom, under ruder or purer form, the Divine Idea of the Universe is pleaded to manifest itself."—*Carlyle*.

"That nothing may be between you and God, but Christ."—*George Fox*.

PREFACE TO THE FIRST EDITION.

The Author has long believed that a popular sketch of the Life and Work of George Fox was wanted. His noble labours in the Gospel, and the many excellences of his character are not known as they deserve to be. The story of his life is full of dramatic interest, and the author has endeavoured to tell it with sympathy and yet with faithfulness.

Too few outside the Society of Friends are aware of the great and happy change which has lately come over it. The cramping influence of custom and precedent is yielding to the free spirit which first made the Society a power. In the present remodelling of its "Practice and Discipline," the study of its early days is of great importance. And for a fervent and constraining piety, for free and large-hearted devotion to "the truth" wherever it leads, few men are more worthy of study and imitation at the present day than George Fox.

Should this effort prove a success, companion sketches of Penn and Barclay will shortly follow.

The Manse,
Batheaston, near Bath;
September, 1883.

PREFACE TO THE PRESENT EDITION.

That "a popular sketch of the Life and Work of George Fox was wanted," was proved by the sale of 1500 copies of this pamphlet within six months of its publication. The opinions expressed by competent judges made me feel that I had not laboured in vain. Ministers of various denominations wrote to thank me, and to confess that they had not understood George Fox before.

This Second Edition contains little that is new, but in the sketch of Barclay will be found several extracts from Fox's letters hitherto unpublished.

GEORGE FOX,

THE

FIRST OF THE QUAKERS.

THE Protestant Reformation was at once a revolt against the claims of Popery, and an assertion of the authority of the New Testament. In neither particular did it satisfy the early Quakers. In their opinion it retained some remnants of Popery to its great disfigurement, whilst it was timid and halting in its acceptance of some of the teachings of the Christian dispensation. They regarded it as their work to reject the forms and ceremonies and "priestly pretentions" that had been retained, in order to reproduce the spiritual worship and simple church life of the apostolic days. Especially they believed themselves raised up to assert the living presence of Christ with his church by his Holy Spirit. They protested that feeble life, however orthodox its creed, was as dishonouring to Christ, and as unworthy of these days of the large outpouring of the Holy Ghost, as was formalism itself. The first and chief exponent of these views was George Fox.

George Fox was born at Fenny Drayton, in Leicestershire, in 1624. His parents were pious members of the Church of England, and he tells with satisfaction that his father was generally denominated "righteous Christer," whilst his mother sprung from "the stock of the Martyrs."

His religious life seems to have commenced almost in infancy. His childhood and youth were marked by a sober bearing, a precocious thoughtfulness, and a love of solitude, which made many notice him; and it was proposed to make him a clergyman. Accordingly, Nathaniel Stevens, the parish priest, seems to have regarded him hopefully, until his deepening experience made the youth aware how blind his guide was, when the former friend became a bitter persecutor. But as some of George's friends objected to his entering the church, he became, in the mingling of businesses so common in that day, shoemaker and shepherd, excelling in the latter contemplative employment, which his friend, William Penn, regards as a fit emblem of his future work. Though he had received only the plainest English education, yet the keen cravings of his strong mind, together with his earnest Bible-reading and much careful thought, soon made him at home in Christian truth, the great topic of conversation and theme of discussion in that age. A noble, severe truthfulness foreshadowed his future teachings, and indicated the stamp of the man. It "kept him to yea and nay," refusing all asseveration or other strengthening of his statements, excepting his favourite "verily." But people remarked that if George said "verily" it was impossible to move him. His own strict and pure life made him feel keenly the poor living of some who made great professions.

But his great preparation for his future work was soon to begin. In his 20th year, his soul began to be racked with conflicts, the nature and source of which he could not understand. This crisis in Fox's history is generally spoken of as his conversion. In some respects it resembles more the deepening and intensifying of a life which already existed. His spiritual nature was waking up to vigorous life. The slight and ill-grasped views which had satisfied the boy did not satisfy the man. They seemed to give no real and sufficient answer to his questionings. He wanted to understand the meaning of life, the plans of God, and his own part in them. In religion he felt that there should be the clearest and strongest mental grasp, insight into the very heart and core of things. He had only seen as in a mist. Where was the seer that could show, by his apt and living words and his accent of conviction, that the veil had been lifted up for him, and that he had verily seen the Shekinah? To such a one he would listen reverently if he could find him; all others seemed mere triflers to his earnest mood. Then again, if God was a real Father, he felt that real and close relations with him must be possible, but he sadly owned that he did not enjoy those relations, and asked himself and others "Why am I thus?" He began to look facts intently in the face, to find out their meaning. He looked at himself and saw only sin; he looked into the professing church, and even there saw the same sad sight. It made him ask, was the gospel a mistake and Christ powerless? Or was he worse than others that his soul should be in such darkness and distress? Was he worse than in former days when he enjoyed comfort, and when the Lord shewed him some of his truth? Had he sinned too deeply to be allowed to enjoy peace? Had he sinned against the Holy Ghost?

In his anguish, like a good churchman he went to his vicar, and asked him to explain his condition to him, but he could not. Then he sought other clergymen, who had a name for strict living or wisdom, but they could give him no help, though he went as far as London in the quest. Some of the advice which he received, he mentions with a pity that is keener than the severest sarcasm. One bade him sing psalms and chew tobacco; another wished to bleed him, but his large frame had been brought into such a condition by his distress, that no drop of blood would flow from him. Such blindness was not peculiar to the clergy. His friends proposed to relieve his sorrows by excitement, and by diverting his attention. Some recommended him to marry, but he sadly replied he was but a lad and must gain wisdom. Others would have him enlist and seek diversion in the exciting events of the civil war; but says Marsden, the historian of the Puritans, "though the bravest man in England, perhaps, if moral courage is bravery, he detested the business of the soldier. Far other thoughts possessed his mind. He had been religiously educated by Puritan parents of the Church of England, and he was now awaking to the consideration of his eternal state."

Meanwhile he fasted often and searched the Scriptures with desperate earnestness. He wandered in solitary places, and spent hours in the trunks of hollow trees in meditation and prayer. Disappointed in the clergy, he turned to the dissenters with no better success. Evidently the thing was of God, for he missed men like Baxter, who could have given him at least good counsel and Christian sympathy. Fox was for some time in Coventry, in 1643, when Baxter was preaching there, one part of the day to the garrison, and the other to the civilians. But possibly if they had met, Baxter's hatred of heresy might have overborne his charity, and obscured his spiritual vision, and he might have branded Fox as a heretic, just as he afterwards dubbed his followers "malignants." *

---

*A similar experience is to be found in the unpublished memoir of that pious and accomplished Quakeress, Miss P. H. Gurney, p. 43. "I was painfully struck with the want of any sign of true devotion or spiritual mindedness in the several congregations I attended in London, both in preachers and hearers. Had I gone, as I once felt some inclination to do, to that called St. Mary Woolnoth, (Jno. Newton's) I might have found an exception to this description; but being accidently prevented, I have sometimes thought it was in the ordering of Providence that whatever of spiritual religion was then circulating in the national church, I was not permitted to find it, though I sought it with the most earnest desire of success." Miss Gurney took these facts as a proof that God intended that she should turn Quakeress; but surely the true explanation of these providences is that God will have us look to Him, and not rest unduly on any man or human system. He spoils our idols that we may worship only Him.

Every experienced pastor must have met with such cases. Until God satisfies the soul the words of men are vain; when His hour has come, the truth which brings light and peace is often one that has been explained and urged before. George Fox had to learn that it is God's work to enlighten, that there is still to be enjoyed a real guidance of the Holy Spirit, resulting in the solution of difficulties and mysteries, in a clear apprehension of the truth, and a soul-satisfying sense of its power. And if the lesson was slowly and hardly learnt, it resulted in a clearer insight into the truth, and more fitness to deal with other tried souls.

At times during these days of trial the dark clouds broke, and for a time the sun shone through. But until he learnt that Christ was to be his Teacher and Comforter, it was but for a time. It was a short respite to gather strength, a brief foreshadowing of the coming joy. Hear his touching thanksgiving for the goodness that did not break the bruised reed. "As I cannot declare the misery I was in, it was so great and heavy upon me, so neither can I set forth the mercies of God to me in my misery. Oh! the everlasting love of God to my soul when I was in distress. When my torments and troubles were great, then was His love exceeding great. Thou, Lord, makest the fruitful field a wilderness, and a barren wilderness a fruitful field. Thou bringest down and settest up. Thou killest and makest alive. All honour and glory be to Thee, O Lord of Glory. The knowledge of Thee in the Spirit is life." But the clouds finally passed away, and abiding sunshine settled on him, when Christ revealed Himself to him as the Great Physician, for whom he had been longing so earnestly. His troubles had lasted three years, and, no doubt, had been aggravated by his morbid fears and mistaken loneliness. But through life his nature was keenly susceptible; for example, the sins of the nation at the Restoration made him blind and seriously ill with grief, in spite of active work and much society. No wonder then that his anguish wore him out at the time when his soul was in the dark, and when that which appeared to him alone worth living for seemed denied him. But now that he was weaned from trusting in an arm of flesh, came the time of divine deliverance. "When all my hopes in them (the dissenters) and in all men were gone, so that I had nothing outwardly to help me, nor could I tell what to do, then, O! then, I heard a voice which said, 'There is one, even Jesus Christ, that can speak to thy condition,' and when I heard it my heart did leap for joy. Then the Lord did let me see why there was none upon the earth that could speak to my condition, namely, that I might give him all the glory. For all are concluded in sin and shut up in unbelief as I had been, that Jesus Christ might have the pre-eminence, who enlightens and gives grace, faith, and power. Thus when God doth work who shall let it? And this I knew experimentally. My desires after the Lord grew stronger, and zeal in the pure knowledge of God and of Christ alone, without the aid of any man, book, or writing. For though I read the Scriptures that spake of Christ and of God, yet I knew Him not but by revelation, as He who hath the key did open, and as the Father of Life drew me to His Son by His Spirit."

This discovery was to Fox what the unfolding of the great doctrine of justification by faith was to Luther. It was not only the commencement of a new life, it was the theme of his life-long ministry, and the special message which he was raised up to deliver to the world. In neither case was there the revelation of a new truth, only an old truth was to be emphasized, and to take its right place in the minds and hearts of men.

To this grand truth, that Christ is still with us to guide us by His Holy Spirit into all truth, Fox henceforth trusted to clear up all doubts, and to unfold all truths, and to explain the Holy Scriptures. So in our day has Mr. Moody set forth prayer as the all-sufficient practical commentator on the Bible. Henceforth, Fox expected Divine prompting to every service and Divine guidance in its performance, and without these he would not move. He had already been convinced of several points afterwards prominent in Quakerism, especially that no place or building can properly be called "holy ground," and that a University training was not a sufficient qualification for the ministry. As to the last point, just as the modern Quaker apostle, Stephen Grellet, said he could no more make a sermon than he could make a world, so did Fox protest against a man-made minister. As he was ever the enlightened and persistent advocate of sound education, this contention must not be mistaken for a contempt of human learning in its right place. It was but an emphatic assertion that the only availing spiritual knowledge comes not through human teaching but through the teaching of the Holy Spirit; and that, on the other hand, where He calls a man to the office of the ministry, the absence of a scholastic training was an utterly insufficient reason for interfering with the call. The abundant blessing which attended the preaching of Fox, Bunyan and other "unlearned and ignorant men," gave emphasis to this doctrine in that age. To these views the other Quaker "testimonies" were speedily added, and soon the whole scheme of doctrine was complete in his mind.

Two points must here be insisted upon:—1st, neither George Fox nor any of the early Friends, though their language is sometimes hazy, ever claimed to be inspired. Says a recent authority, [Fielden Thorp, B. A., in the Friends' Quarterly Examiner for April, 1870,] "It has often been a cause of satisfaction to us that nowhere in the authorised documents of our society is the word (inspiration) applied to the ministry of Friends." Secondly, notice that Fox was most careful to note how his convictions corresponded with Holy Scripture. So he says, "When I had openings they answered one another, and answered the Scriptures, for I had great openings of the Scriptures."* Whilst, then, the fallibility of the ministry is acknowledged, and the infallibility of the Bible asserted, surely the doctrine of the Divine Guidance is not perverted through insufficient safeguards. But we are not prepared in all points to defend Fox's application of the doctrine. Possibly he sometimes mistook the workings of his own mind for the promptings of the Holy Spirit. Nor are his theology and his interpretations of Scripture beyond criticism. His ideas on the Divine In-dwelling took the form of the famous doctrine of the Seed or Light within. But though the teaching and guidance of the Holy Spirit are taught by Friends as distinctly as ever, it is questionable whether the doctrine of the Light within *in the precise form in which Fox preached it, and Barclay developed it theologically,* has obtained the general acceptance of the Society. It certainly is not to be found in its authorised publications, such as the official "Doctrine, Practice and Discipline." It speaks well for the independence of thought in the society, that the pet-child of its great leaders should be abandoned when it failed to secure their conscientious assent.†

---

* The following passage from an American life of George Fox, coming from a reliable Quaker source, corroborates this assertion. Speaking of the early Friends the writer says :—" Their belief in a divine communication between the soul of man and its Almighty Creator, through the medium of the Holy Spirit, by which the Christian may be 'led into all truth,' did not at all lessen their regard for the authority of the Holy Scriptures *as the test of doctrines.* They constantly professed their willingness that all their principles and practices should be tried by them; and that whatsoever any, who pretended to the guidance of the Spirit, either said or did which was contrary to their testimony, ought to be rejected as a Satanic delusion; and also, that 'what is not read therein nor may be proved thereby, is not to be required of any man that it should be believed as an article of faith.'" Page 357.

† The reader will not mistake this for an assertion that Friends have surrendered the doctrine of the Divine guidance and indwelling. For a fuller discussion of the question see the close of the sketch of Barclay.

Since Macaulay so grossly caricatured Fox, it has been assumed that Penn and Barclay added to Fox's ideas whatever was meritorious in Quakerism. On the contrary, not only the theology of the society and its polity, but also its philanthropy and its enlightened views on religious liberty, must be ascribed to him as their chief exponent. If the Quakers object to call him their Founder, it is only because they wish to honour God, rather than the human instrument. They never hesitate to give him his due, nor do they falsify their own teachings by seeking to win favour for them by great names. There is no clearer testimony than that of Penn, that Fox's services received full recognition in the Society during his life-time. Indeed the position accorded him moved the envy of some, in spite of his own meekness and humble carriage.

Fox's personal spiritual experience may be regarded as the laying of the foundation-stone of Quakerism. Now let us turn to the rearing of the superstructure. Having learnt where to look for help and enlightenment, his heart soon found rest. His bodily strength returned, and his mind as well as his soul received a vast impulse. He seemed to have a sympathetic insight not only into the hearts of men, but also into the secrets of nature, so that at one time he questioned whether he ought not to practice medicine. To the end of his life he remained an ardent lover of nature and of science, so that his friend, William Penn, calls him "a divine and naturalist too, and all of God Almighty's making." But soon he settled down to his true life-work as an itinerant preacher of the gospel. His patrimony was sufficient to enable him to devote himself freely to the work. In his wanderings in search of light, he had made the acquaintance of many anxious seekers after truth. To these he naturally went in the joy and ardour of his heart, to tell them what God had taught him; and many of them received "the truth." His first convert was a woman,

Elizabeth Hooton, who also became the first lady preacher in the new Society, and after much service died in the West Indies, whilst accompanying Fox and others on a preaching tour. Soon we find him preaching in ordinary congregations, and in the conferences common in that day, and gaining a name for spiritual discernment.

Though but a youth of 23 when he began to preach, there was a spiritual power attending his ministry that was remarkable. Macaulay speaks of his "chant" in preaching; many Welsh preachers now "chant" the gospel with great effect, and the recitative in Mrs. Fry's ministry was acknowledged to be wonderfully impressive. But it must not be supposed that it was deliberately chosen, it is probable that he fell into it unconsciously. The intensity of his emotion too added to the impression; his large frame quivered and shook with his strong feeling. Charles Lamb has given a vivid description of what he calls "The Foxian orgasm:" probably the description would accurately apply to Fox. We can judge from his Journal how keen and penetrating his appeals must have been, and how exultant his praises and thanksgivings.

Then again he preached, not metaphysics, nor formal theology, but a living, present Christ. He told his experience with pathos and power. No wonder that people wept and laughed for joy, for they felt it was true glad tidings that he brought. His word was literally "in power and in the Holy Ghost, and in much assurance," and many received it as the word of God to them. Soon his converts were numbered by hundreds. In 1647 he first began to preach publicly, and in that and the next year several "meetings" were gathered.

Any one who passes along the East Lancashire Railway from Colne to Burnley, must be struck by the towering grandeur of Pendle Hill; and if he climbs it, he will be rewarded by a glorious panorama. Whilst looking on this magnificent view, George Fox tells us he had a vision, in which he saw that this region would be the home of thousands of Quakers; and certainly nowhere did Quakerism find such a stronghold, and receive such sturdy helpers and gifted preachers. Alas! the glory has departed! Partly as the result of extensive emigration, many of the meeting-houses then so full of devout worshippers are now empty, whilst in some others a formal few, whom Fox would hardly acknowledge as his followers, meet in cold silence sabbath by sabbath.

Fox did not long work single-handed; in a few years, especially from this district on and about the Penine Range, a band of preachers gathered round him whom Quakers still delight to honour. In 1654 he tells us there were sixty preaching in all parts of England and Wales. Some of his helpers had been ministers, like Francis Howgill and John Audland. But it was not taken for granted that they would still preach, unless there was the manifest call. Thus Thomas Lawson, a clergyman at Ramside near Ulverston, a man of considerable learning, seems to have relinquished preaching when he was converted by Fox. He was a great botanist, and says Sewell, "one of the most skilful herbalists in England," so he seems to have gained his livelihood by this skill and by tuition. Yet the authoress of "The Fells of Swarthmoor Hall" calls him a man of fervid eloquence, so that it was not lack of gifts that kept him from preaching, but it must have been the persuasion that he was not called to the work. So in our own day, that master of eloquence, John Bright, though a man of strong religious feeling, never preaches, in spite of the freedom which Quakerism allows.

Besides clergymen and other ministers, the converts included magistrates, like Justice Hotham and Anthony Pearson, author of "The Great Case of Tithes;" and officers in the army like Col. West and Capt. Pursloe, besides gentlemen of substance and standing like I.

Pennington, and scholars like Samuel Fisher and Thomas Lawson just mentioned. But among them all Fox stood chief, not only as the father of the fathers among them, but also in his firm and clear grasp of the truth, his entire devotion, his gifts of leadership, his many labours and sufferings, and his God-given success. "I notice," says a contemporary letter, "that in any company when George is present all the rest are silent;" and a joint letter by Edward Burrough and Francis Howgill says, "Oh but for one hour of his company! what a treasure it would be to us!" Even those who had held similar views before they met with him, often gained from him more clearness of view and fulness of knowledge.

The manner of conducting the Quaker "meetings for worship," was the result of practical conviction rather than of theory. They thought that for Christians to meet together in order to go through a stated form of service, was at once to cramp the outpouring of the heart to God, and to interfere with the Holy Spirit in his direction of the utterances of Christ's ministers. When they met in silence, each could speak to God what was in his heart, and each could hear in his spirit "what God the Lord would speak;" and if any one was "moved" to declare any truth, the way was clear. Thus Christ was owned practically as a present Lord, and the Holy Spirit trusted as a real and practical guide. They read in their New Testaments that when the saints met together, all the gifted might prophesy one by one as anything was revealed to them; and that each might contribute to the service his psalm of thanksgiving, or hymn of adoration, or edifying doctrine. It seemed to them that in the "apostacy" of the churches not only the rights of private Christians, but the claims of the Holy Spirit had been interfered with by the "one-man ministry." And probably none of them, whatever his gift of discernment, imagined in those days of burning zeal and abundant labours, that the time would come when their simple system would prove a rigid bond, which would leave half their meetings without ministry of any kind. Encouragement of a true ministry is as needful as discouragement of the spurious.

Very early in the history of the Society, the distinguishing views of Friends on the Sacraments were clearly enunciated. In 1656, Fox sent out a manifesto clearly stating his views, especially on the Lord's Supper. He thought the outward rites were simply adaptations of Jewish customs, temporary condescensions to the weakness of the converts from Judaism until the destruction of Jerusalem, and even during that period, optional, not obligatory. If the early Christians kept up the old custom of sipping the wine and breaking the bread, then they must do it in remembrance of Christ's death, and not of the deliverance from the bondage of Egypt. But he believed the outward rite Jewish in its style, and foreign to the pure spirituality of Christianity. So also with regard to Baptism.*

There were two kinds of service which the devoted leader rendered to Christian truth—he preached it with zeal and unction, and he suffered for its sake. His sufferings were unquestionably often the result of his own unwisdom. Many Friends themselves now lament his want of a conciliatory spirit. He could not put himself in the place of others, so as to see how they viewed himself, his conduct and his claims. Thus he was constantly led to impute dishonest and impure motives to others if they did not agree with him. All but his own unpaid ministers were "priests" and "hirelings" and so on. But nothing can justify the treatment he received, often through the connivance, sometimes from the instigation, of clergymen and magistrates. Whitefield's hootings and peltings were nothing, in comparison

---

* The other leading "testimonies" of Friends were against all war, and against oaths, even in a court of justice.

with Fox's stonings, and brutal beatings, and horrible imprisonments. As Marsden says, "He rebuked sin with the authority of a prophet, and he met with a prophet's reward."

We must remember in extenuation of his admitted faults that he aimed to be a reformer, appealing afresh to first principles in conduct, and seeking to arouse others to feel their force. He purposely set himself against mere conventionalism, especially when it fostered pride or cloaked some rottenness in society. When persecuted, he never resorted to flattery or depended on wheedling, but appealed to conscience and to the humane or Christian feelings which ought to have been in the breast of the persecutor.

He proved to the full the power of passive endurance. Smitten on the one cheek, he literally turned the other. He believed that a large share of his work for the Master was in the testimony of suffering, and he was more anxious to be obedient than to avoid what seemed to him the pains and penalties of obedience. He would not walk out of prison unless he could do it not only honourably, but conscientiously, satisfied that he was not flinching from his appointed testimony. He truly gloried in afflictions for Christ's sake. While refusing to honour an unchristian statute by keeping it, he bore patiently and unresistingly the legal penalties, unshaken in his loyalty to the government and unsoured in his disposition towards mankind. But further, Fox clearly saw that endurance was sure to end in victory, and he inspired his friends with the same conviction. "The more they imprison me," he writes triumphantly, "the more the truth spreads." In the same spirit said William Penn at a later date, "I will weary out their malice. Neither great nor good things were ever attained without loss and hardship. The man that would reap and not labour must perish in disappointment." No wonder that men grew weary of punishing those who endured in this spirit. No wonder that the lofty conscientiousness of the Quakers was felt to be the salt which had a large share in counteracting the corruption of the Stuart reigns, and in preserving our civil and religious liberties. Says Orme in his Life of Baxter, "The heroic and persevering conduct of the Quakers in withstanding the interferences of government with the rights of conscience, by which they finally secured those peculiar privileges they so richly deserve to enjoy, entitles them to the veneration of all the friends of civil and religious liberty." And again he says, "Had there been more of the same determined spirit among others which the Friends displayed, the sufferings of all parties would sooner have come to an end. The government must have given way, as the spirit of the country would have been effectually roused. The conduct of the Quakers was infinitely to their honour."

Meanwhile Fox abounded in labours, sparing no exertions to make known the truth and to plead for righteousness. He sought a purer life as much as a purer faith. He went into public houses to plead for temperance, and into fairs to plead for uprightness and honesty, and into courts to plead for justice, as well as into churches to plead for spiritual religion. We must not forget that in those fermenting times it was no uncommon thing for questions and remarks to be thrown at the preacher during divine service, and it was considered quite in order for any one to address the people after the clergyman had finished his sermon. Thus when Fox was speaking in the Ulverston Church, Justice Sawrey cried, "Take him away," but Margaret Fell interposed, "Let him alone; why may not he speak *as well as any other?*" So that these interruptions were not considered so strange and disorderly then as they seem to us now. But public feeling was against the man and against the truths he preached, and to that public feeling he could not and would not yield. He could not take off his hat before the great, for that was an honour which he reserved for God alone. He felt bound to protest against all flattering titles and speeches, which, though the world counts them harmless civilities, seemed to his sober spirit and delicate conscience such as should neither be given nor received by the followers of the lowly Nazarene. His "thee and thou," and plain speaking, and sober dress, and keen rebukes, brought on him a perfect storm of anger and abuse. He felt that he stood in the forefront of the battle against worldliness, and bore the brunt of it; and he was meekly thankful for such an honourable post.

His first imprisonment was at Nottingham, for interrupting divine service; but he had his triumph, the very Sheriff was converted, and compelled by his new-found zeal to go forth into the market-place, and take up the imprisoned preacher's work. His second term soon followed at Derby, on a charge of blasphemy. He believed in the doctrine of perfection, and told those who opposed him that they pleaded for sin. The Derby Magistrates asked him if he was sanctified, and he answered, "Yes." "Then they asked me if I had no sin? I answered 'Christ my Saviour has taken away my sin and in Him there is no sin.' They asked how we knew that Christ did abide in us? I said, 'By His Spirit that he has given us.' They temptingly asked if any of us were Christ? I answered, 'Nay, we were nothing, Christ is all.'" Yet they found him guilty of blasphemy, confounding him with the fanatical, antinomian Ranters. But if he taught perfection, Oh! how he lived! Let those that reject his teaching excel, or at least equal, his living. In Derby, his jailer was converted, to strengthen and comfort him in his sufferings. Whilst in prison his busy pen poured forth many letters of advice to Friends, and "testimonies" against all forms of iniquity, including war and capital punishment.

Before he was 27, Fox had passed through more

varied experience than many have in a long lifetime. Honour and revilings, converts and imprisonments, love for the gospel's sake and cruel beatings by the mob, nearly ending in death—these had already been his portion. But his work was now bearing much fruit. In one twelve-months, 1650-1, he gained such staunch helpers as Richard Farnsworth, James Nayler, William Dewsbury, Justice Hotham, and Captain Purslow. Soon afterwards the Fells of Swarthmoor were led to Christ by his preaching and became the most devoted of adherents. Soon his followers could be numbered by thousands. It was not the strength of his arguments that gained them; the age was overdone with reasoning. Fox mocked their syllogisms with grim humour. There was a wonderful spiritual power about him. He spoke naturally, with simple, direct earnestness, and overwhelming vehemence, right to the conscience of the hearers. He made people both listen and understand him, and feel the power of the truth in a way which many did not like. He was a wonderful evangelist. What his cultured convert, Isaac Pennington, the Rutherford of Quakerism, said of Friends generally, is applicable to him. They might offend his taste and move him to contempt by their intellectual poverty, but they compelled him to respect their spiritual power and their deep acquaintance with the things of God.

Then again the new Society was a real brotherhood. The members stood shoulder to shoulder as fellow servants of the one Master. Their only emulation was which should do most and suffer most cheerfully. Their great question was "Lord, what wilt Thou have me to do? Where wilt Thou have me to go?" The Jesuit was ready to go at an hour's notice wherever the Pope sent him. The Quaker was as ready in his obedience to the voice within. Not only Great Britain, but Italy, Turkey, Syria, and Egypt heard the truth before 1662. John Stubbs, "a remarkable Oriental scholar," and

Henry Fell, who was also "well versed in Arabic and Hebrew," set out for the land of Prester John, but were stopped by the English Consul at Alexandria. Their leader was chief simply through gifts and devotedness. So strongly were Friends attached to him that when he was in Launceston gaol, one of them went to Cromwell and offered to lie in prison in his stead; which made the Protector turn to those around him and ask, "Which of you would do as much for me if I were in the same condition?" And Fox showed himself worthy of such devotion by always seeking the post of danger and the most arduous work. Urgent he might be, for he was tremendously in earnest, but to speak as Hepworth Dixon does of his "imperious instincts" simply shows ignorance of the man.

For centuries no such zealous and noble-spirited evangelism had been seen. No wonder that it won its way. Many who had been rich, like Isaac Pennington, were content to become poor by fines and distraints for "the truth's sake." Most nobly did they help each other. If they did not insist on community of goods as a theory, they carried out the spirit of it in practice.

There are two marked stages in Fox's work; first the Evangelistic Stage, and then the Organising Stage, which was, of course, overlapt by the other. Let us trace the salient points in his evangelistic work. In 1654 he was brought before Cromwell, and made a good impression on that keen judge of men. His sincerity stood testing, his zeal for God was manifestly genuine, and the grand, though not faultless Protector, learnt heartily to respect him. As he was turning to leave him, Cromwell caught him by the hand and said, "Come again to my house, for if thou and I were but an hour of a day together, we should be nearer one to the other." Next year he visited him again, to lay before him the ill-treatment to which Friends were subjected.

The meetings now gathered, wherever "the man in leather breeches" went were immense. At one in Bristol, he tells us, 10,000 people were present, and often 2000 or 3000 are mentioned as collecting to hear him. The energetic evangelist often had periods of grudged but not useless interruption of his labours by imprisonment. Indeed, as Mr. W. E. Forster says, he "would have been qualified to draw up a report of the state of the gaols of the Island, so universal and experimental was his acquaintance with them." But his imprisonments did not make him cease from labour. He wrote innumerable letters and tracts, and he preached the gospel to those that came to see him with such effect, that one of Cromwell's Chaplains said they could not do him a greater service for spreading his principles in Cornwall, than to imprison him in Launceston gaol.

In 1656 occurred the sad episode of James Nayler's fall. He had been one of the most popular of the Quaker preachers, and had enjoyed the warm friendship of Fox and other leaders. But extravagant praise turned his head so far that he listened to blasphemous songs and invocations addressed to him by excited women, allowed them to kneel before him, and even to welcome him to Bristol with a horrible parody of our Lord's triumphal entry into Jerusalem. These miserable proceedings he did not like, but he excused them as honors done, not to him, but to Christ his Lord. The way in which Fox and other Friends acted in this matter was most praiseworthy. Many of the enthusiasts who misled Nayler were not truly Friends at all, and yet the Society was credited with fanaticism on account of their proceedings. Their enemies exulted in a clear case against them, and the religious world seemed justified in regarding them with suspicion. But in spite of all this, the Friends clung to the deluded man, and tried every means to open his eyes. George Fox visited him in Exeter gaol, and used every power of reason and persuasion, and at last finding he could do nothing with him, sadly gave him to understand that their friendship was at an end, and that Friends could no longer regard him as one of them. Yet still they visited him, and tried hard to gain the Protector and Parliament to their humane view of the right way of dealing with the case, and they had their reward. The cloud that obscured his mental vision passed away, and he deeply and truly repented of his sad error. He published a full recantation, took upon himself the whole blame, absolving the Society from all share; and endeavoured in every way to undo the mischief he had done. But whilst their love and gentleness had thus conquered, the barbarous spirit of the age had vindicated orthodoxy, by passing and executing the horrible sentence of branding and tongue boring. And it is sad to think, that the man who endured this torture was already a repentant man, won by love, not by severity, to confess and renounce his sin. The Quakers at once received him into full confidence and esteem, and helped him, in truly Christian fashion, to bear the results of his fall. Thus early in their history, in the midst of an age of much persecution and bigotry, were established those habits of loving Christian discipline, which have so nobly distinguished the Society ever since. But the reclaimed wanderer was not long allowed to continue his resumed preaching. In the summer of 1660 he was taken ill, and died in his 44th year.

In the same year 1656, Fox tells us that more than 1000 Friends were in prison for conscience sake. But though he had not been long out of prison, and was in continual danger of arrest, he would not relax his labours. He extended the range of his evangelistic efforts into Wales, and gained a rich harvest there, as he had before amongst the equally fiery-souled Cornish men. The style of his own preaching may be judged from his exhortation to his fellow-ministers, penned whilst in

Launceston gaol. "Dwell in the power, life, wisdom and dread of the Lord God of life and heaven and earth, spreading the truth abroad, awakening the witness, confounding the deceit, gathering up out of transgression into the life, the covenant of light and peace with God. Let all the nations hear the sound by word or writing. Spare no place, spare no tongue nor pen. Go through the work, and be valiant for the truth upon earth." How like Wesley's assertion that the world was his parish. Like him, Fox might have boasted that his followers were *all* at work, and *always* at it. Like Wesley, too, he wrote as he travelled, by which alone we can account for the wonderful amount that he wrote. He had no gift for literary composition; his spelling was erratic, and his sentences, like Paul's, were long and involved, probably because they both dictated their letters hastily to some secretary. But if his letters bear marks of haste, they are pithy, and pointed, and full of gracious unction. Any spiritually-minded Christian may greatly enjoy his fervent appeals and powerful statements of Gospel truth. His letters and tracts served the practical purpose for which they were intended, and he was satisfied.

The year 1657 saw him enter Scotland, where he had a presentiment that a glorious vintage was to be gathered. He was met by determined opposition from ministers and others, who smelt heresy in his teachings, especially as he was an Arminian. What they hated in him may be seen from the following curses, which, in the fiery style of that age, were pronounced in kirk, the people pronouncing the response. "Cursed is he that saith, Every man hath a light within him sufficient to lead him to salvation: and let all the people say, Amen. Cursed is he that saith, Faith is without sin: and let all the people say, Amen. Cursed is he that denieth the Sabbath-day: and let all the people say, Amen." But for all this terrorism, within ten years there was a body of Friends in Scotland, that, by their earnest piety, and solid consecrated learning, gladdened the heart of the devoted leader.

The troubled times after the death of Cromwell tried Friends in many ways. The Committee of Public Safety sought to induce them to join the army, many of them having been brave and efficient soldiers before their convincement, but they unanimously refused. Attempts were made to identify them with the Fifth Monarchy men, and other disturbers of the public peace, for they were disliked by almost every one; but the prudence and energy of Fox and others avoided these snares, and gained the confidence of the powers that were.

When Charles II. ascended the throne he proved even more friendly than Cromwell had been. Dr. Stoughton says, "Charles had a sort of liking to the Quakers for their harmlessness and their oddity. He was not afraid of their taking up arms against the throne, and to quiz them in their queer dresses and with their quaint speech, was to him a piece of good fun." It suited the merry Monarch to have pretty Quakeresses like Sarah Fell coming with their petitions, enduring his bantering demurely, and going away delighted with the clemency he so often showed. In 1666 he granted the release of George Fox from the sentence of premunire. He had once before set him at liberty, only to fall again into the clutches of the law. In March, 1664, Fox had been brought before Justice Twisden, and after a sham trial that was an outrage on both law and humanity, the extreme sentence of the law in such cases, the sentence of premunire, was passed, and he languished in Lancaster gaol and Scarborough Castle for nearly three years But at last the royal ear was gained, and Fox, ill with hard treatment in the foul cells at Scarborough, was restored to his liberty, his property, and his civil rights. In prison he had been busy writing in exposition of the views of Friends. After his release, for some time he was principally engaged in modelling the discipline and church government of the Society.

Before passing on to consider the organisation of the Quaker community into a compact and well regulated church, we must notice their conduct in the question of marriage. "Marriage," said Fox, "is God's ordinance," believing literally the common saying that marriages are made in heaven. But the solemn compact ought to be publicly ratified, and what more fitting than that public worship should attend that celebration. If Fox denied that ministers could marry, if he insisted that the ceremony should consist simply of a mutual pledge publicly given, he was very careful that all should be done in good order. The marriage customs which obtain amongst Quakers to-day represent his views. The young people must show that they are clear of other marriage engagements, and have the consent of their parents or guardians to their union. Sufficient public notice must be given of the coming event, so as to prevent all scandal and disorder. Then the marriage is celebrated during a week-day service. In the early days of the Society the publication of the intended marriage was no easy matter. "Many a joke must have passed through the merry crowd, when, from the market-cross of a country town, the expecting bridegroom proclaimed his forthcoming nuptials—but no arrangements of a loose or evasive character, would have saved the marriages of Friends from the double brand of public opinion and of national law." In 1661 the legality of Quaker marriages was tested in Nottingham before Justice Archer, and the point was forever set at rest.

Now let us turn to the work of Fox in the organisation of the Society. That the organisation was principally planned and carried out by him is past all doubt. We will quote two out of numberless authorities. Marsden says—

"To understand Quakerism the reader must comprehend the character of George Fox; for no institution ever carried more thoroughly impressed upon it the features of its chief."—*Marsden's Christian Churches*, p. 424.*

T. Hancock says, in his prize essay on the causes of the decline of Quakerism—

"The master spirit and chief builder of Quakerism was undoubtedly George Fox. . . When we come to the second period, to the modelling of the Quaker constitution and discipline to the Society of Friends, to Quakerism as an *ism*, the hand of George Fox is still more evident."—*The Peculium*, pp. 68, 69.

The views of Fox as to the church polity were exceedingly simple. He had no intention of forming a sect; he only met the needs of his friends, as the exigences of the hour dictated. The less machinery the better; the simpler the arrangements the more they commended themselves to his judgment. His mind was not hampered by theories. His aim was to recognize the gifts of all, and not to have the life bound by man's rules.

But there must be discipline in the church. The disorderly must be dealt with. The weak must be helped. Many were thrown into prison or even banished; they must be relieved or cared for in the best way their circumstances allowed. Many had lost all for conscience sake; they must not be allowed to want. None so full of pity for these sufferers, as he who suffered so readily himself. Almost his last words were, "Remember poor Friends in Ireland."

The New Testament was his only conscious rule, prayerful waiting upon God for light his only expositor

---

* For this quotation and other valuable matter the writer is indebted to the writings of Alderman Rowntree, of York, whose "Two Lectures on George Fox" and prize essay on "Quakerism, Past and Present" are standard works on Quakerism.

of it. He might ask his learned friends for side-lights from church history, might ask them about the practice of the early church, or the history of the corrupting influence of certain false doctrines. But he was emphatically a man of one book, and he read that book with his heart, more than with his penetrating mind.

That competent authority in all matters concerning Quakerism, Mr. J. S. Rowntree, thus describes the origin and progress of the Quaker discipline. "With the rapid growth of the Society, George Fox increasingly perceived the necessity for taking steps to repress the outbursts of fanatical and misguided zeal, and for placing the government of the church on a more systematic basis. This decision was undoubtedly expedited by the occurrence of a heresy fomented by John Perrott. . . He had the satisfaction of seeing most of Perrott's adherents make a public acknowledgment of their error, and immediately afterwards, he initiated a national system of disciplinary meetings, to be held monthly. They consisted of the most experienced Friends within a given district; and had the charge of the affairs of the body within such district. The Quarterly Meetings (many of which we have seen were already in existence) were gradually put on a different basis, and consisted henceforth of representatives fron a number of associated Monthly Meetings, whose decisions in some cases were liable to revision by the superior meeting. It was not till a somewhat later date that a central body—the 'Yearly Meeting' of London—consisting of representatives from all the Quarterly Meetings in the country, was established as the top stone of this elaborate disciplinary system. . . . To the settlement of these Monthly Meetings, George Fox most assiduously devoted himself in 1667–68; and ere long, wherever meetings for the worship of God were held after the manner of Friends, little church synods were also held, ministering to the wants of the poor, alleviating the sorrows of the prisoners, seeking to reclaim disorderly walkers, and when failing in this, disuniting them from the body." ("Two Lectures on Macaulay's Portraiture of George Fox," pp. 40-42.) It speaks volumes for the sagacity of Fox that so little has needed to be added to or altered in the Quaker polity since his day.

In 1666 the Barclays joined the society, and in the next year William Penn was added to their number. The learning of Robert Barclay, and social position and administrative ability of William Penn, were soon appreciated by the leader with whom they worked so loyally.

In 1669 Fox visited Ireland, and in the same year he was married to Margaret, widow of Judge Fell, of Swarthmoor Hall. She had been one of his early converts, and was one of his most vigorous helpers. She wrote almost as many letters, and printed almost as many appeals as her husband; she visited the imprisoned, and sent relief to their families. Her house was the home of all Quakers visiting the neighborhood, and her purse was at the service of all who needed money to serve the cause. Her judgment was reliable and her energy untiring; she was the Countess of Huntingdon of the Society. She even endured long imprisonments, and risked, and for a time endured, the loss of all her property by premunire for the truth's sake. She was therefore a fitting helpmeet for George Fox. She had four daughters who were ministers in the Society, and the whole family regarded him with reverence, except the scapegrace elder son. He not only opposed the marriage, but with the basest ingratitude, he endeavoured, after it was accomplished, to turn his mother out of her own home; and he rests under at least grave suspicion of being a party to the plot to have her sentenced to premunire.*

---

* The penalties of this sentence were, to be put out of the King's protection, to forfeit lands and goods to the King, and to be liable to imprisonment for life or at the King's pleasure.

Fox acted throughout this affair with the greatest prudence and magnanimity. He would not even be suspected of seeking worldly gain, but carefully secured to his wife and her family, the property which was hers before their marriage. No wedding could be more simple than his own. "Afterwards," he says in his journal, "a meeting being appointed on purpose for the accomplishing thereof, in the public meeting-house at Broadmead in Bristol, [the site cannot now be certainly determined,] we took each other in marriage. . . . Then was a certificate, relating both the proceedings and the marriage, openly read and signed by the relations, and by most of the ancient Friends of that city, besides many other Friends from divers parts of the nation." Evidently the ceremony caused considerable excitement. His wife was ten years his senior.

But of home life they had little enough; in little more than a week they parted, that the husband might continue his labours, and soon after, the wife was cast into prison, where she remained until 1671. Then through the intercession of her daughters with the king she was released, and the premunire, which had rested on her for ten years, was removed. They had a few days together before Fox sailed for the West Indies, and again on his return, and so on.

Men and women who give their most intense and sustained sympathies to christian enterprises, often have to suffer for it in their home relations. "We were very willing both of us," says Mrs. Fox after her husband's death, "to live apart for some years upon God's account and His truth's service, and to deny ourselves of that comfort which we might have in being together, for the sake of the service of the Lord and His truth; and if any took occasion, or judged hard of us because of that, the Lord will judge them, for we were innocent."

In the summer of 1671, George Fox and some other Friends visited the West Indies and the continent of

America, to push the work of evangelisation and of organising the societies there. They landed in Barbadoes, after a voyage enlivened by constant dangers from the leakiness of the vessel, and once by an almost miraculous escape from capture by a Sallee man-of-war. Fox's son-in-law, John Rous, was in the company, and on landing he was at once taken to the house of Mr. Rous, senior, who was a wealthy sugar planter. Fox's health had been so injured by the ill-usage which he had endured at different times, and he suffered so keenly from the climate, that he had to remain at Mr. Rous's, whilst his friends held meetings all around. But though crippled in body his mind was vigorous. The marriage regulations and discipline of the Society, and the duty of giving Christian instruction to the negroes, engrossed his attention. The question of slavery stirred his heart to its depths; and his vigorous language and action not only did good then, but laid a right foundation for the future action of the society. When the time came that Friends had to consider the question of the abolition of slavery, few things exerted so much influence in the right direction, as Fox's clear statement of the issues involved. His words were quoted, his reasonings were expanded and enforced, and it was largely through his influence that abolitionist principles became identified with Quakerism.

Here, as elsewhere, the doctrines of the society had been greatly misrepresented, so the famous letter to the governor of Barbadoes was drawn up to explain them. It is still often quoted as an admirable statement of the views of the society. It is as near an approach to a creed as anything can be, which originated from a society which recognises only the Bible as authoritative, and which objects to all human formularies.

The society in Barbadoes gained greatly in numbers and strength by this visit. Jamaica, Maryland, North Carolina and Virginia were next visited in the same manner and with similar results. Large numbers were won to a christian life. The Indians and negroes were recognised as having a claim to christian sympathy and religious instruction. The societies were weeded of unworthy members, and their organisation successfully accomplished. Then the party returned in safety to England after an absence of a year and a half.

In 1677 Fox carried these operations into Holland, having with him his illustrious friends, Penn and Barclay. "This visit of the three great apostles of Quakerism," says Hepworth Dixon, "seems to have made a great sensation; scholars, merchants, government officers, and the general public crowded to hear them preach, and the houses of the most noble and learned men in the city of Van der Werf and Erasmus were thrown open to them freely. . . . Their journey through the country was like a prolonged ovation." The interesting episode of the interview with the enlightened and large-hearted Princess Elizabeth, granddaughter of James I., scarcely belongs to this sketch, as Fox did not join in it. But he wrote a lengthy epistle of Christian counsel, and sent it by his daughter-in-law, Mrs. Yeamans, and the Princess returned him this brief but kindly reply:—

"Dear Friend, I cannot but have a tender love to those that love the Lord Jesus Christ, and to whom it is given, not only to believe in Him, but also to suffer for Him; therefore your letter, and your friend's visit, have been both very welcome to me. I shall follow their and your counsel as far as God will afford me light and unction; remaining still your loving friend, Elizabeth."

He spent some time in Amsterdam "writing in truth's account," and then returned home by Harwich. In 1684 he paid another visit to Holland, the last of his longer missionary journeys.

After this, finding his health shattered by his long

imprisonment and arduous labours, he settled down in London, quietly, though not uselessly, awaiting the end. His correspondence was most extensive, and he wrote many tracts and pamphlets as was his habit. One of his last letters was written to the lately-bereaved widow of Barclay, the Apologist, and is a model of Christian consolation. He tells her:—"Thou and thy family may rejoice that thou hadst such an offering to offer up unto the Lord as thy dear husband; who, I know is well in the Lord in whom he died, and is at rest from his labours, and his works do follow him." He signs himself one "who had a great love and respect for thy dear husband, for his work and service in the Lord, who is content in the will of God, and all things that he doeth—and so thou must be." But besides this literary work, he laboured zealously in the pastoral work, visiting the sick and afflicted, and endeavouring to "bring into the way of truth such as had erred."

He watched the passing of the Toleration Act with the deepest interest. It was a most welcome relief to Friends, especially those in Ireland. The losses sustained by the Irish Quakers were enormous. In one year (1689) they were estimated at £100,000, many being stripped of all they had (see Besse's Sufferings). George Fox not only collected such facts as these for publication, but, even in his last days of suffering and prostration, attended at the House of Commons to interest the members in the sufferings of his brethren, and to see that the Toleration Act was "done comprehensively and effectually."

He was equally zealous in his attendance on public worship. When so infirm that he could hardly sit through a service, he would not desist, and often afterwards had to lie down on a bed until recruited. He was determined, if possible, to die in harness, and God gave him his heart's desire.

He was especially anxious lest spiritual religion

should decline, now that persecution had ceased, and Friends began to prosper in business. He wrote them an epistle of loving, but earnest expostulation, warning the young against the fashions of the world, and the old against the deceitfulness of riches. To the latter he pointedly says, "Take heed that you are not *making your graves* while you are alive outwardly." To some ministers who had gone to America he writes similar stirring words of counsel:—"And all grow in the faith and grace of Christ, *that ye may not be like dwarfs;* for a dwarf shall not come near to offer upon God's altar, though he may eat of God's bread that he may grow by it."

On the Sunday preceding his death, he preached with great power at the meeting in Gracechurch Street, but soon afterwards had to take to bed, complaining of cold and weakness. His wife had been to see him some little time before, and finding him enjoying better health than usual, was unprepared for his death, so that no near relative seems to have been with him at the time of his decease. It was indeed a consecrated chamber. Those who stood round him were struck with the triumph of faith over bodily weakness. He exulted in the power of Christ. "All is well—the Seed of God reigns over all, and over death itself." His thoughts were calmly fixed on the arrangement of Society affairs; his mind was clear, his habitual disregard of his bodily sufferings still marked him. Towards the last all pain left him. Feeling death coming, he closed his own eyes and extended his limbs; and in sweet composure, resting on Christ his Saviour, his spirit entered into rest on Tuesday, 13th December, 1690 (o.s.)

Three days after, some 2000 persons (one witness says 4000) gathered to lay him in his grave. For two hours they worshipped in that same meeting-house in Gracechurch Street, in which he had preached only on the previous sabbath. William Penn, George Whitehead,

Stephen Crisp, and other leaders amongst them, thanked God for the gifts and services of their departed leader, and exhorted and encouraged each other to faith in that Lord, who raised him up and sustained him in his work. Then the body was conveyed to Bunhill-fields, and interred in the Friends' Burial Ground there.

On the day of his death, William Penn wrote to Swarthmoor to tell the news of his decease. His letter reminds us of the inscription of the Carthaginians on the tomb of Hannibal. "We vehemently desired him in the day of battle." He sadly says to Mrs. Fox, " I am to be the teller to thee of sorrowful tidings, which are these:—that thy dear husband and my beloved friend, George Fox, finished his glorious testimony this night about half-an-hour after 9 o'clock, being sensible to the last breath. Oh! he is gone, and has left us with a storm over our heads. Surely in mercy to Him, but an evidence to us of sorrows coming. . . . My soul is deeply affected with this sudden great loss. Surely it portends to us evils to come. A prince indeed is fallen in Israel to-day!" and in a postscript he adds, "He died as he lived, minding the things of God and His church to the last, in a universal spirit."

Fox's Journal was published soon after his death, with a lengthy preface by his friend William Penn, containing a warm tribute to his personal worth and christian labors. The Journal gives us a better and more vivid idea of the man than any biography that has been written. An intelligent and liberal-minded Baptist minister thus describes the impressions it left on his mind:—

Rev. Wm. Rhodes to his wife:

"'My dear heart in the truth and the life which are immortal and change not;'

"So George Fox usually addressed his wife. I have finished his life of 650 folio pages since you have been gone. It afforded me much amusement, but its chief impression is that of the highest veneration and delight, for so holy and noble a servant of Christ. I have hitherto regarded Penn as the most beautiful character which that sect has produced, and perhaps it is the most beautiful, because his mind was more polished and cultivated than that of his friend; but Fox's character is by far the most venerable and magnificent. He reminds me of the inspired Tishbite in his stern majesty and fidelity, but he seems to have surpassed him in all the patient, gentle, compassionate, suffering, laborious virtues. If inspiration has been granted since the apostles departed from the world, I think he possessed it. I have read few things more truly sublime than some of his letters to Charles II."—*Memoir of W. Rhodes, Jackson and Walford, p.* 179.

Ellwood, the friend of Milton, has left us a glowing testimony to the value of George Fox's Life and Work. But the eulogies of William Penn and Thomas Ellwood are not portraits. One of the best estimates of his character ever given to the world is that by J. C. Colquhoun in "Short Studies of some Notable Lives." In it he says (p. 88–90) :—

"The truth is that Fox's character had, like that of many others, two sides; and the contrast between these is so great that one can hardly believe them to belong to the same man. On the one side we have strange thoughts and words, fanciful imaginations, the illusions of an unlettered mind. But such things are not unusual. Dr. Johnson believed in second sight, in dreams and ghosts; and his case presents to us the credulity of a child, with the intellect of a giant.

"But if we turn to the other side of Fox's character, we find this man of fancies and visions confronted with controversialists, Jesuits, and lawyers, puzzling them with his subtlety, and with his logic beating down their fence. Now in a court of justice he confronts the judge, defies the bar, picks flaws in the indictment, quotes against them adverse statutes, and wrings from baffled judges a reluctant acquittal. Then he is in the Protector's court, to meet a man hard to dupe. There he plants himself, his hat on his head, at Oliver's dressing table, engages him in long discourse, sets before him his duty, presses on him the policy of toleration, till the iron-hearted soldier, first surprised, then attentive, at length interested, extends his hand to the Quaker, bids him repeat the visit, and tells him if they could meet oftener they would be firmer friends.

"No less remarkable are his courage and skill. As storms thicken, he is always in the front of the battle; wherever the strife is vehement there he is; now in Lancashire, now in Leicester, in Westmoreland or Cornwall; meeting magistrates and judges, braving them at Quarter Sessions, vanquishing officers, governors of castles, and judges. Then he sits down calmly to organise, with a forecast equal to that of Wesley, the scheme of Quaker polity which has lasted to our times. And if we smile at the oddity of his language, at the curious missives which he hurls at mayors and magistrates, jailors and judges, we find at times a caustic style worthy of Hudibras or Cobbett, in which he lashes the frippery of the court, or meets the casuistry of the Jesuits or Ultra-Calvinists; and as we dwell on those words of wisdom in which he tells us of his faith, and cheers the heart of Cromwell's daughter, we perceive that he is no common man, but one who, with strange training and singular notions, rose by the strength of genius and piety to a wide command over men."

But though honoured by the Society which he founded, Fox has not received his due from the religious world in general, nor from the friends of civil and religious liberty. It is significant that whilst his friend, William Penn, has found at least three respectable biographers outside his own sect, Fox has found but one; and whilst Penn has been defended again and again from Macaulay's charges, the only defence of George Fox against his groundless sneers that is well-known, is from the vigorous pen of Mr. J. S. Rowntree. Fox has received scant justice from all but "Friends;" *their* loyalty, as we have seen, has been beautiful, unfaltering and enthusiastic. Most writers seem to have been too much afraid of his peculiar views, and repelled by his uncouth style, to be just to his large heart and mind, and to his wonderful services as an evangelist. The man who advocated general education, who was anxious that Philadelphia should have a botanical garden, who battled for perfect religious liberty, who pleaded for the rights of the negro and for the reform of prison discipline, who organised the polity of Quakerism, and associated philanthropy inseparably with its system, was a remarkable man, far in advance of his age, and worthy of more regard from the country that has been so greatly blessed by his labours.

Lord Macaulay has thought fit to speak of George Fox as not mad enough for Bedlam, but too mad for liberty, as "not morally or intellectually superior to Ludovic Muggleton or Joanna Southcote," he has termed his journal "absurd" and his letters "crazy." Unfortunately, Hepworth Dixon, whilst correcting Macaulay's gross misrepresentations of Penn, has confirmed those concerning Fox. He speaks of his spiritual struggles with a sneer, credits him with "imperious instincts," and is evidently ashamed that Penn was in any way allied with him. It will, therefore, be simple justice to Fox, to ask the reader who may be prejudiced against him, by the vigorous epithets and dashing portraiture of the historian, to set against his caricature some opinions of men less biassed, and well worthy of confidence. Let him remember that if Macaulay speaks with unmeasured contempt, Kingsley, Carlyle, and a host of others speak of Fox with respect.

And first, as to his Journal, listen to the words of

Coleridge and Sir James Mackintosh. Coleridge in his *Biographia Literaria* observes:—"There exist folios on the human understanding and the nature of man which would have a far juster claim to the high rank and celebrity if in the whole huge volume there could be found as much fulness of heart and intellect as bursts forth in many a simple page of George Fox."

Sir James Mackintosh describes his "absurd" book as "one of the most extraordinary and instructive narratives in the world, which no reader of competent judgment can peruse without revering the virtue of the writer, pardoning his self-delusion, and ceasing to smile at his peculiarities."—*Miscell's Works*, vol. II. p. 182.

Is not the testimony of these witnesses preferable to the manifest prejudice of Macaulay?

Now as to George Fox's powers of mind and high moral character, place against Macaulay's sarcasm the good opinion of other competent judges. We will not quote the elaborate eulogy of Ellwood, the friend of Milton; of William Penn's warm tribute we will only quote the saying that he had never seen him "out of his place, or not a match for every service or occasion." But these were personal friends. Let us hear others. Marsden in his "Later Puritans," speaks of his "penetrating intellect." The accomplished Alfred Vaughan speaks thus of Fox, in what Charles Kingsley calls his "fair and liberal chapters on Fox and the early Quakers," in his "Hours with the Mystics:"—

"Oppression and imprisonment awakened the benevolent, never the malevolent impulses of his nature,—only adding fervour to his plea for the captive and the oppressed. His tender conscience could know no fellowship with the pleasures of the world; his tender heart could know no weariness in seeking to make less its sum of suffering. He is a Cato Howard. . . . In the prison experiences of George Fox are to be found the germs of that modern philanthropy in which his followers have distinguished themselves so nobly. In Derby gaol he is "exceedingly exercised" about the proceedings of the judges and magistrates, concerning their putting men to death for cattle, money, and small matters,—and is moved to write to them, showing the sin of such severity, and, moreover, what a hurtful thing it was that prisoners should lie so long in gaol; how that they learned badness one of another in talking of their bad deeds; and therefore speedy justice should be done. . . . As to doctrine again, consider how much religious extravagance was then afloat, and let us set it down to the credit of Fox that his mystical excesses were no greater."

The historian Bancroft says:—"His fame increased; crowds gathered like flocks of pigeons to hear him. His frame in prayer is described as the most awful, living, and reverent ever felt or seen; and his vigorous understanding, soon disciplined by clear convictions to natural dialectics, made him powerful in the public discussions to which he defied the world. . . . The mind of George Fox had the highest systematic sagacity."—*Bancroft's History of the U.S.*, Vol. II. pp. 508-9.

But finally let us appeal to the high authority of Carlyle, who estimated truly the spirit and aim of Fox's life. There was much in common between them in their sturdy love of truth and reality, leading to a hearty hatred of empty forms and mere conventionalities. Both had a striking directness of thought and purpose, going right to the heart of things; an intense earnestness that did not stop nicely to weigh words, but hit hard at all unrighteousness. There was in both a strong sense of personal responsibility that made them indifferent what others might think or do. Carlyle gives us in "Sartor Resartus" (Popular edition, pp. 144, 5) a striking eulogium on George Fox, from which we will select the following characteristic passage:—" Perhaps the most remarkable incident in modern history is not the diet of

Worms, still less the Battle of Austerlitz, Waterloo, Peterloo, or any other battle; but an incident passed carelessly over by most historians, and treated with some degree of ridicule by others; namely, George Fox making to himself a suit of leather. This man, the first of the Quakers, and by trade a shoemaker, was one of those to whom, under ruder or purer form, the divine idea of the universe is pleased to manifest itself; and across all the hulls of ignorance and earthly degradation, shine through in unspeakable awfulness, unspeakable beauty on their souls; who therefore are rightly accounted prophets, God-possessed, or even Gods, as in some periods it has chanced."

The length of these quotations needs some apology; but the influence of the vigor and cleverness of Macaulay's caricature needs to be counteracted; and the confidence with which he pronounces judgment will doubtless lead many unwary readers to accept his opinion. It should at least be known that men equally able, and more competent to estimate a nature like Fox's, have admired his character and valued his work. But after all the best testimony to his worth is contained in the devoted life which we have been endeavouring to sketch.

WILLIAM PENN,

THE

FOUNDER OF PENNSYLVANIA.

PREFACE.

The story of William Penn has been told so often and so well that it is impossible to introduce novelty into it without introducing falsehood. This Macaulay found out to his cost, his representations doing more to expose his liability to prejudice than to damage the stable reputation of Penn. No wonder such a beautiful and eventful life has attracted many biographers. If Clarkson did not possess all the information that is now in existence, he is accurate and sympathetic. Hepworth Dixon is brilliant but not always accurate, and he fails altogether in the religious portion of his story from utter want of sympathy and insight. In Dr. Stoughton both these qualities are joined to that broad acquaintance with the religious history of the age which is so essential to the just portraiture of such a man. He has added to the biography many interesting details. Dixon complained that the memoirs of Quakers are transcendental and lacking in human interest. No book can deserve the censure less than Dr. Stoughton's life of Penn.

WILLIAM PENN,

THE

FOUNDER OF PENNSYLVANIA.

WILLIAM PENN was born in London, in 1644. His father was the famous but time-serving admiral Sir William Penn; his mother, Margaret Jasper, the beautiful and intelligent daughter of a Rotterdam merchant. His father's ambition was high. He had gained wealth and the royal favour by his daring and ability; his son should work out a grand career, and should be a peer, Viscount Weymouth. But man proposes, God disposes. The stout Admiral lived to find the strong, handsome, quick-witted child, on whom he built so much, a very sword in his soul, the last stroke that brought down his proud self-willed nature to the very dust before God, and made him at last think seriously of that religion which he had despised when in health and gaiety.

The child of such hopes received a careful training. First, he was sent to Chigwell School in Essex, which was near the home of his childhood at Wanstead. After that, he entered Christchurch College, Oxford, where he met some of the friends of his after years, including Robert Spencer, afterwards Earl of Sunderland, and John Locke. Already, signs of strong religious feeling had manifested themselves in the boy. When a child at Shangarry Castle, a Quaker preacher—Thomas Loe, destined to play such a prominent part in his history—came to Cork. His father, little suspecting the results that would follow, invited him to the Castle, and gathered the neighbours to hear him. His preaching deeply impressed the whole gathering; it made Sir William weep freely, and left an impression on the mind of his child-hearer which was never effaced. That impression was deepened by a singular vision which he had at Chigwell School. "Alone in his chamber, being then eleven years old, he was suddenly surprised with an inward comfort, and, as he thought, an external glory in the room, which gave rise to religious emotions, during which he had the strongest convictions of the being of a God, and that the soul of man was capable of communication with Him. He believed also, that the seal of Divinity had been placed upon him at this moment, or that he had been awakened, or called upon to a holy life." Again at Oxford, he was greatly influenced by Dr. Owen, with whom Penn corresponded when he was removed from his position as Dean, to make way for a more pliable instrument of the schemes of the court.

Penn's attainments were already considerable for his years, yet his College course was doomed to be a failure. The most noteworthy occurrences in it were, his again hearing the Quaker preacher, Thomas Loe, and his vigorous opposition to the Ritualistic innovations of the Stuarts. The authorities insisted on the gown being worn by all under-graduates. Penn and others, recognising this as the thin end of the Popish wedge, not only would not wear it themselves, but tore it from the backs of those who did. This led to his expulsion for rioting.* His father was most annoyed at the disgrace attending the punishment, until he found that his son's conduct resulted from settled convictions, already firmly rooted. Then the Admiral at once understood the serious issues involved. He must vanquish these conscientious scruples or his ambitious plans would be ruined.

---

* He tells us that his expulsion resulted from his writing a book, which "the priests and masters did not like." Probably both reasons were combined.

He never planned a sea-fight more carefully. In the first moment of anger he had soundly whipped his son, and turned him out of doors; now he tried gentler and more insinuating means. Like a true man of the world, he had full confidence in the power of a gay life to cast out such thoughts, and he sent his son to Paris. The most interesting incident of the trip is his treatment of a French gallant, who insisted on fighting him over some supposed insult. In vain did Penn politely explain that no insult had been offered. They must fight. Penn not only excelled in athletics, but was a skillful fencer. He soon disarmed the man, but instead of then punishing him for his quarrelsomeness, he only returned him his sword with a polite bow.

Sir William Penn, delighted with what he heard of the success of this expedient, determined that his son should finish his education in France, after which he destined him for the army. But in God's providence, the chosen tutor, the learned divine Moses Amyrault, if he did not deepen the gracious impressions already received, grounded him thoroughly in theological studies, which were very useful to him afterwards. Leaving him, Penn travelled for some time, and returned home, says Pepys, "a fine gentleman." He then studied law awhile in Lincoln's Inn, and to good purpose, as we shall see.

The great plague of 1665 drove him from London, and probably revived his serious thoughts, which were further strengthened by intercourse with serious people and the reading of serious books. His father again remarked the dreaded relapse, and again tried what change would do. This time he sent his son to Ireland, to the sprightly court of the Lord Lieutenant, the Duke of Ormond. Again, he reckoned without his host. There were Quakers in Ireland, and the very plan to which the astute Admiral trusted to get his son out of danger, led to his joining their Society. At first, indeed, nothing seemed less likely than such a result. He was beginning to despair of finding "the Primitive Spirit and Church upon Earth," and was ready recklessly to give himself up to the glory of the world. He was so flattered by the cordial recognition of the spirit and the success with which he assisted in quelling a petty insurrection, that he was inclined to fall in with his father's plan, and adopt the profession of arms. He even went so far as to apply for a captaincy. But God had other things in store for him. Happening to hear that Thomas Loe, the Quaker by whom he had been so impressed in Oxford, was visiting in Cork, he went to hear him. His ministry is said to have been singularly lively and convincing. The sermon was wonderfully suited to Penn's case, and made him weep much. The opening sentence cut him to the quick: "There is a faith that overcomes the world, and there is a faith that is overcome by the world." From that night he determined that, by God's grace, his faith should not be overcome by the world. He began to attend Quaker meetings regularly. At one of these, in November 1667, a soldier came in, and made a great disturbance. Penn, like Phineas in "Uncle Tom's Cabin," not having yet thoroughly subdued the old nature, took him by the collar, and would have thrown him down stairs, had not Friends interfered. The soldier went away, and gave information to the authorities, who came and broke up the meeting, haling several, including Penn, before the magistrates.

His cavalier dress, so unlike that of his companions,[*]

---

[*] He did not at once adopt the Quaker dress, and continued for some time to wear a sword. When this non-compliance with Quaker customs was reported to George Fox, it is said that he simply replied, "let him wear it as long as he can." He mentioned years afterwards how the peculiar garb was a stumbling-block to some, "It telleth tales, it is blowing a trumpet and visibly crossing the world; and this the fear of man cannot abide" (*Travels*, p. 121). Probably this very fact commended the peculiarity to his bold and decided spirit.

led the mayor, before whom the party was taken, to offer to release him upon bond for his good behaviour. Penn denied his right to demand such bond, and challenged the legality of the arrest. When committed, he appealed to his friend the Earl of Orrery, Lord President of Munster, by whom he was speedily set at liberty. But that gentleman wrote the news to his father, who at once summoned him home. He reasoned, he stormed, then, proud and haughty as he was, he condescended to plead. Finally, finding his son still unyielding, and hearing complaints of his preaching at different meetings in town and country, he turned him out of doors, telling him also that he should leave his estates to those that pleased him better. He was then twenty-three years of age.

Henceforth William Penn's time and strength were given to Quakerism. There was neither hesitation nor half-heartedness. The welfare, work, and sufferings of Friends he made his own. He wrote and preached with untiring energy, and suffered, counting it joy.

Though turned out of doors by his father, he was not allowed to want. His mother privately supplied his needs to the utmost of her ability, and what she could not do was made up by several kind friends. The situation was painful in the extreme; separated from home and parents, his father grieved and mortified at his conduct. He tells pathetically afterwards of "the bitter mockings and scornings that fell upon me, the displeasure of my parents, the invectiveness and cruelty of the priests, the strangeness of all my companions, what a sign and wonder they made of me." But his conscience approved of the line he had adopted, and his resolute nature was troubled by no waverings. He set himself earnestly to do his duty. He united himself closely to the Friends, and took up his pen on their behalf. His first work was entitled "Truth exalted."

"The Guide Mistaken," soon followed. It was a

reply to "A Guide to the true Religion," in which the Quakers were treated with great severity.

Shortly afterwards he was drawn into a public discussion with the Rev. Thomas Vincent, a Presbyterian minister in Spitalfields. Some of his congregation having become converts to Quakerism, Vincent said some slanderous things about the Friends. So George Whitehead and Wm. Penn waited upon him, and insisted that as he had publicly misrepresented them, he was bound in fairness to give them an opportunity publicly to set themselves right. After some demur, Vincent agreed to meet them in his own chapel on a certain day. The discussion lasted until midnight, and turned principally upon the question of the Trinity. Friends have always asserted that the doctrine, as taught by the orthodox, is an attempt to explain the inexplicable, and goes beyond what is revealed in the Scriptures. This contention in their early days cost them much reproach; now the chief remnant of it is the annoyance of having their authors, especially Penn, quoted as believers in the Unitarianism of to-day.

The debate was one-sided and bitter, and the Friends only retired at last on condition of having another opportunity to vindicate themselves. But as Vincent plainly showed that he had no intention of redeeming his promise, the only satisfaction left was the press. In "The Sandy Foundation Shaken," Penn gave the public his view of the matter. But he did not stop with the doctrine of the Trinity, he went on to the Atonement. He advanced such arguments against "Imputed Righteousness" as Barclay has elaborated in his Apology. He also produced arguments against the method in which in those days the necessity of a satisfaction to the Divine justice was taught. His expressions unfortunately resemble those of modern Unitarians, but his position is vitally different. Penn believed the death of Our Saviour on the cross a real Sacrifice, that "Jesus

Christ was our holy sacrifice, atonement and propitiation, that he bore our iniquities," but that Christ is not the cause but the effect of God's love. (See his "Primitive Christianity revived.")

This book brought down on Penn the anger of Dr. Sanderson, Bishop of London, and led to his being sent to the Tower. But that only "added one more glorious book to the literature of the Tower," "No Cross, No Crown," of which Hepworth Dixon, more trustworthy in literature than in religion, says, "Had the style been more condensed, it would have been well entitled to claim a high place in literature." Whilst there he also replied in a treatise entitled "Innocency with her open face," to many strictures on the "Sandy Foundation Shaken."

This imprisonment revealed in two ways the stuff of which William Penn was made. First severity was tried, and one day his servant brought him the report that the bishop was determined he should recant or die in prison. He only smiled and said, "They are mistaken in me; I value not their threats. I will weary out their malice. Neither great nor good things were ever attained without loss and hardship." Then they sent Stillingfleet, the future bishop, to try his powers of persuasion, but they, too, utterly failed. "Tell my father, who I know will ask thee, that my prison shall be my grave before I will budge a jot, for I owe my conscience to no mortal man." Such spirit, combined with the ability his books were revealing, revived the admiral's pride in his son. The court, too, began to take interest in him, and shortly after Stillingfleet's visit he was released, having been in the Tower more than eight months.

He at once resumed his preaching, and having been partially reconciled to his father, was employed by him to attend to his Irish estates. On his return home, his father received him fully into his favour, to the great delight of his mother's heart.

But soon trouble again overtook him, though only again to place him on a pedestal where his virtues and power would be more manifest, and where his voice would reach a larger audience. Going to the meeting-house in Gracechurch Street, London, he found it closed and guarded by soldiers. However the Friends held their service in the street, and for this W. Penn and W. Meade were indicted under the Conventicle Act. Hepworth Dixon regards this as "perhaps the most important trial that ever took place in England," and speaks of Penn as the great vindicator of the old charters and of trial by jury. He met the browbeating of the city magistrates with spirit and dignity, and encouraged the jury to do the right manfully. After twice returning an evasive verdict, and being locked up for forty-eight hours, the jury finally acquitted the prisoners. The court was greatly annoyed, and vindictively fined the jury for contempt. They refused to pay the fine and were sent to prison. Penn encouraged them to test the legality of this imprisonment, and the highest legal authority in the land decided against it and released the gallant jury.* A full account of the whole proceedings was published, and helped materially to encourage resistance to illegal interference with liberty.

But important as this trial undoubtedly was, the full benefit of it was only secured by long years of bitter sufferings endured by the whole Quaker community. (See sketch of Fox.) Let us who enjoy the spoils remember gratefully those who fought the battle.

We have spoken of the marked individuality in William Penn's character which led him to continue to wear the court costume after he became a Friend, until his own conscience demanded that he should adopt the

---

* In his second trial "Lord Chief Justice Vaughan pronounced his noble vindication of the right of jurors to deliver a free verdict, which by giving independence to juries, made the institution so effectual a protection to the liberty of the subject."—W. E. FORSTER.

Quaker garb. The same individuality led him to diverge from the ordinary type of Friend in another and more important matter. They were bent on fighting out the battle of religious liberty by religious, rather than by political weapons. They might, when on trial, quote a statute or plead a precedent as a sort of argumentum ad hominem, but in political and constitutional affairs, as such, they as a class took no delight. Penn was an exception. He felt a keen interest in the political affairs of his country. He saw that it was a mistake to lose the benefit of the old charters and statutes which secured the liberty of the subject, and he appealed to them on all occasions. This appeal served two purposes. It acknowledged the civil duties of Christians, which some Christians are slow to recognise. It also secured the sympathies of many in their struggles to whom the religious aim was incomprehensible. Both these objects seemed to Penn of the highest importance; they influenced his whole career. In the words of W. E. Forster, "the form of his religion, his feelings as a Quaker, did not seem to him to interfere with the fulfilment of his duties as a citizen. Had it done so, that form would have been changed rather than the work left undone, for he was not a man to make one duty an excuse for shirking another; within his conscience there was no conflict between religion and patriotism; he did not fly from the world, but faced it with true words and true deeds."

Admiral Penn was lying on his death-bed whilst this trial was in progress, and it added greatly to the sufferings of his son, that he could not be with his father at such a time. But on his release he hastened home, and very touching was the final converse between father and son. The high spirit was humbled; the worldly heart had learnt the emptiness of earthly honours. "Son William," he said only a day or two before his death, "I am weary of the world. I would not live my days over again if I could command them with a wish, for the snares of life are more than the fears of death. This troubles me that I have offended a gracious God. The thought of this has followed me to this day. Oh, have a care of sin! It is that which is the sting both of life and death." We can imagine with what feelings the Christian son would hear this tardy confession, and would endeavour to point such a father to the source of his own hopes and consolation. The old sailor was buried with due honours in the fine old church of St. Mary's, Redcliff, Bristol. He left the bulk of his property, some £1500 a year—a great sum in those days—to his eldest son, who thus found himself in spite of the risks he had run for conscience sake, a wealthy man, able to devote money as well as time and strength to the cause of his adoption. The king and his brother, the Duke of York, afterwards James II., had promised the dying man to be guardians to his son—a promise sought by him because he foresaw the many troubles into which that son's conscientious scruples would lead him in such an age. This fact is the key to the relations in which William Penn and the royal brothers often stood to each other—relations otherwise puzzling, but creditable to both sides when thus explained. The Stuarts were faithful to this promise when interest pointed another way. Penn was true to James especially, in spite of faults which greatly tried him; true, even when his throne tottered, and finally fell.

The Penns had an ancient family seat in Buckinghamshire. Not far away at Chalfont lived William Penn's friend, Isaac Pennington, and his wife, and his step-daughter, Gulielma Maria Springett. There also lived Thomas Ellwood, quaintest of Quaker rhymesters, and his great master, Milton. No wonder Penn found the place attractive. But the great attraction soon came to be Guli Springett, beautiful and spirited and accomplished, and yet a true Quakeress. He had met her first at a friend's house where he called when returning to his father's house, to the interview which ended in his expulsion from home. Her father was Sir William Springett, who was killed at the early age of twenty-three, after a chivalrous defence of Arundel Castle for the Parliament. Guli was born a few weeks after his death. After losing her husband, who like most of the best officers of the Parliament was a staunch Puritan as well as a good soldier, Lady Springett passed through a time of great spiritual unrest. At last she found a home amongst the Friends. She afterwards married Isaac Pennington, attracted to him by the spiritual ties of a similar religious experience. They were both examples of the numerous class of those who were almost Quakers before they were aware that such a Society existed. In 1672, William Penn made Guli Springett his wife. The interval after his father's death had been filled up by writing several books, preaching, holding a public discussion with one Jeremy Ives on the universality of the Divine Light, a short visit to Holland, and of course the inevitable imprisonment, six months in Newgate for attending Wheeler Street Meeting.

In his wife he found a true help-meet, both in piety, zeal for Quakerism, and large-minded sympathy with all Christian and patriotic causes. He loved her deeply and tenderly, and found in her love the brightest feature of his chequered life. After his marriage he had a long, sweet rest, and then plunged deep into work again.

He visited the Court, for the first time since his father's death, to plead for George Fox's liberty. It was an errand on which for the next fifteen years he was often to go. He seems to have had a wonderful power of drawing out the best side of the royal brothers; and no nobler sight can be pictured than the courtly Friend, hating the court for its worldliness and sin, but frequenting it to speak bold words of truth or gentle pleas for mercy; feeling that his influence there was a trust not to be neglected, but wielding it with constant watchfulness and wonderful self-control. Meanwhile, writing and preaching were not forgotten. Amongst other engagements, he had, in 1675, a public discussion with good Robert Baxter, of which, unfortunately, very few details are preserved. Perhaps, the most competent and charitable opponent of Friends at this time was Dr. Henry More. The combined wit and seriousness of Penn's pamphlets overcame his dislike to controversy, and led him to go carefully through the discussion which he had had with John Faldo. He was also at this time in communication with George Keith, then, perhaps, the most learned defender of the doctrine of Immediate Revelation. The intercourse led to mutual regard and respect. "If thou happen to see Henry More," writes George Keith to Robert Barclay, when the latter was in London, "remember my dear love to him. Notwithstanding of his mistakes, I would have Friends be very loving and tender to him, as indeed I find a great love to him in my heart. But as for his paper I see no difficulties in it at all to weaken in me anything I have written to him."

Before proceeding to speak of the great work of Penn's life, the founding of Pennsylvania, we must anticipate a little to refer to his manifold labours for his own religious Society. His well-balanced nature found no difficulty in rightly blending the sacred and the secular. Whilst electioneering for Sidney, whilst gathering facts and making business arrangements for New Jersey, or taking interest in the Royal Society, his religious life was still full and fervent. At the time that he was living at Worminghurst, almost overwhelmed with business, we are told that his spirit was so warm and eager, that when the Friends assembled for worship, he could hardly wait to reach his seat before beginning to pour forth the fulness of his soul.

He watched with lively interest the work of organisation which Fox was carrying on in so masterly a fashion. When John Perrott caused a disturbance, by refusing to remove his hat whilst praying in public, or William Rodgers obstructed Fox's path, mistaking discipline for tyranny, none were more ready than he to rally round the trusted leader. In 1677, he joined Fox, Barclay, and others, in a visit to Holland, to organise and consolidate the Society there, and to visit such promising enquirers as the Princess Elizabeth, the Countess de Hornes, and the courtly Van Helmont. He published a full and glowing account of the religious services in which they were engaged, which gives us a vivid picture of the "times of refreshing" which the brotherhood enjoyed in its early days.

The next year, 1678, when reports of Popish plots kept the nation in a constant alarm, he was twice heard before a committee of the House of Commons, in support of a petition which he presented on behalf of the Society of Friends. Their inability to take an oath, led to their being caught in the meshes of an Act intended for Catholics. William Penn explained their position with dignity and great candour. With characteristic boldness, though asking for a favour, he did not flinch from pleading for full liberty of conscience even for the hated Papists. The committee listened respectfully, and adopted his suggestions for the relief of Friends; but the sudden prorogation of Parliament prevented the bill from being carried.

It shows the perfect independence of Penn's mind that though he was on good terms with the King, he risked giving offence by his open and hearty sympathy with Algernon Sidney. That patriot, after long years of banishment was allowed to return home in 1677. Soon after, he yielded to the representations of his republican friends, and sought a seat in Parliament. First he tried Guildford, and then Bramber; but was not only hotly opposed by the court, but dishonourably

and illegally tricked out of the seat. All through the
struggle he had the enthusiastic and vigorous support
of Penn, although at the time the affairs of Pennsylvania were far from settled, and he had so much
reason to wish to keep the royal favour. Usually Penn
kept clear of party politics, but on this occasion he canvassed and spoke for his friend with great zeal; so that
the French Ambassador speaks of him and Sidney as
the two trusted leaders of the republican party. But
though Penn's action proves that he did not share the
scruples of most of his brethren against participating in
political affairs, yet it was probably the man and his
principles that won his confidence, rather than the party
with which he acted. Probably, Penn would have en-
dorsed the early opinion of his father-in-law, Isaac
Pennington, who wrote, (1651) "Whoever they are,
whom I saw fitted for it (Government) and called to it,
they should have my vote on their behalf." In the
midst of politics and schemes of emigration, the stream
of his polemical works still continued to flow, and every
year saw one or more pamphlets from his pen.

Turning to his private life, in 1680, he lost his beloved father-in-law, Isaac Pennington. Though gifted
with a refined mind and a loving heart, he had a nature
far less robust and vigorous than his son-in-law, who
shortly after his death edited his collected works. But
a heavier blow followed. In 1682, Lady Penn died,
and her death seems to have made him seriously ill for
some time. She had clung to him when his adoption
of Quakerism turned his father against him, and she
took care of him when he was turned out of doors. She
never accepted Quakerism, yet probably her gentle and
loving nature had an influence with her son that the
stern father never had.

Now begins the story of Pennsylvania. As boy and
youth it had been his favourite dream that in America
might be planted a new England, without the faults of

the old—a home of civil and religious freedom. Events now ripened the scheme. On the one hand, fierce persecution urged him on; England and Germany seemed to be bent on driving out their most energetic and high-souled children. On the other, the way opened gradually and safely. In 1675, he was induced to become a manager of West New Jersey. After five years experience he bought East New Jersey in 1681, and in the same year the King granted him, by charter, the fine tract adjoining, now called Pennsylvania. This was in lieu of £16,000 due to his father for pay, and for money advanced in desperate times to strengthen the navy. We are told that the Admiral obtained the promise of this tract, having heard from a relative glowing accounts of its richness. From the first, the "holy experiment," as Penn called it, was popular. Algernon Sidney, with whom he kept up constant correspondence, and whom he loved as a brother, helped him to sketch a constitution for it. The Quakers, who had long been discussing (especially since George Fox's visit to America in 1672) some scheme of colonisation, were ready to supply emigrants of the right class in large numbers. He had but to publish a sketch of the intended constitution, and a statement of the resources and attractions of the colony, and the response was immediate.

The constitution which he gave to Pennsylvania, and which he spent many of the best years of his life in reducing to practice, has been universally admired. Hepworth Dixon has sought for the genius of it in the experiences of ancient Greece, and in the dreams of More and Sir Philip Sidney. Penn was, indeed, acquainted with these, but his inspiration was found in the instincts and aims of Quakerism. Plato and Sir Thomas More, and even Algernon Sidney, had less to do with his constitution than had George Fox. He found in the Society to which he belonged a body combining a rare amount of freedom with admirable organisation—a Society with abundant elasticity yet with excellent discipline and cohesion. Quakerism not only acknowledges that methods and governments exist for the sake of men, it believes that manhood, especially sanctified manhood, is the great security of liberty and justice. Its aim is to give scope to the individual to live out the dictates of his own conscience, and to contribute his utmost share to the general well-being. We are greatly mistaken if this was not also the aim of Penn in the constitution which he gave Pennsylvania.*

Unfortunately for the perfect realisation of his hopes, such a scheme, like Quakerism, needs grand men to work it. The maxims of Heaven cannot be worked out by the instincts of earth. Had the other Friends in Pennsylvania shared his spirit of lofty self-sacrifice, the story of this State might have been more noble and stimulating even than it is. But from the first, Quakers shrank from the turmoil and cares of official life. But this shrinking only makes more striking the unconquerable spirit that animated Penn. He could suffer and be strong. He could "scorn delights and live laborious days." To the end, he retained the reins of Pennsyl-

---

* "In the constitution of the colony he was assisted by Algernon Sidney, and at Worminghurst and Penshurst the two friends drew up its several articles. That it established perfect freedom of conscience, it is needless to remark. It established also a no less absolute freedom of trade; Penn sacrificing to this desire the sums which he might have received from the sale of monopolies. The constitution was democratic; a council of seventy-two, elected for three years, formed the Senate, which Penn intended to be the deliberative body; an assembly, elected by ballot and universal suffrage, and paid [they received threepence per mile for travelling expenses, six shillings a day while in the assembly, and the Speaker ten shillings a day] confirmed or rejected the Acts of the Council. Trial by jury gave scope to public opinion, but the provision that the judges were chosen only for two years, and could then be removed by the Assembly, impaired the administration of justice. Religion was left to voluntary efforts. [State] education was carefully provided for. The Indians were treated on principles of such manifest justice, that they became the friends of the new Colony, and no Quaker blood was shed by them." Short Sketches, pp. 151-2.

vania affairs in his own hands as proprietor, though he might have got rid at once of his burden of growing debt and of the corroding care, by selling out. But one thing restrained him; says his noble wife, "My husband might have finished it [the deed of surrender] long since had he not *insisted so much on gaining privileges for the people.*" (Logan's Life, p. 56). And so even when the load was crushing him he continued to bear it rather than mar the "holy experiment," the great ambition of his life. This power of resolute and skilful persistence until his ends were gained, had won for his father wealth and honours. He, recognising it as his noblest gift, chose it as the fittest offering which he could place on God's altar. His life thus stands as a rare instance of thankless toil for the honour of God and the welfare of man, persisted in through weariness, suffering, and loss, and resulting in unsurpassed usefulness.

The first band of emigrants left England in 1682, under the charge of Penn's cousin, Colonel Markham, who was appointed Deputy-Governor. Penn himself followed on the 1st of September, landing at Newcastle, on the 27th of October. He left behind him a farewell letter to his wife, full of tender assurances of love, and of wise and highly characteristic advice as to the training of their children. He at once summoned the General Assembly to adopt the constitution he had prepared. "There was little talk and much work in the first Pennsylvanian Parliament. On the third day their session was completed, and Penn prorogued them in person. They had left their ploughs for half-a-week, and had met together and founded a State."

Penn soon won the hearts of the Red Indians. "A lady who lived to be a hundred, used to speak of the Governor as being rather of a short stature, but the handsomest, best looking, lively gentleman she had ever seen." "He endeared himself to the Indian by his marked condescension and acquiescence in their wishes. He walked with them, sat with them on the ground, and ate with them of their roasted acorns and hominy. At this they expressed their great delight, and soon began to show how they could hop and jump; at which exhibition, William Penn, to cap the climax, sprang up and beat them all." No wonder that some of the very staid Quakers thought him "too prone to cheerfulness for a grave 'public Friend,'" that is, a minister of the Gospel. But without that elasticity that led to the ready jest and the hearty enjoyment of simple pleasures, the burdened brain must have collapsed before it did. His was an intense nature, keen both in suffering and in enjoyment, doing with its might whatsoever it found to do.

Shortly after this he concluded his memorable treaty with the Indians—"the only treaty," says Voltaire, "between those people and the Christians that was not ratified by an oath, and that was never broken." "The treaty," says Dr. Stoughton, "was probably made with the Delaware tribes as 'a treaty of amity and friendship,' and not for the purchase of territory." But the details of the story seem wrapped in impenetrable mystery. "The speeches made, the dresses worn, and the surrounding scene, appear now to be altogether fictitious."

A society had been formed in Bristol, called the "Free Society of Traders of Pennsylvania." To them William Penn wrote an account of his province that is now full of interest. Says Dr. Stoughton, "It indicates great power of observation, a wide range of knowledge, much skill in grouping facts, and an unaffected yet vigorous style of description on the part of its author." Besides facts about the natives of the country, he speculates about their origin, and thinks they may be the descendants of the lost ten tribes.

After spending some two years in Pennsylvania and

seeing Philadelphia grow until it had 2,500 inhabitants, William Penn returned home in 1684. He had two special reasons for doing so. He had had many disputes with Lord Baltimore, the Roman Catholic proprietor of Maryland, respecting boundaries, and having failed to come to terms, he was applying to the Lords of Plantations to decide the case. Then again the persecution of the Quakers was very bitter, and he hoped he might be able by means of the royal favour to check its severity. He reached home early in October. As to the persecution nothing was done to purpose until James II. ascended the throne, when 1200 Quakers were liberated from prison. But the credit of inclining the royal mind to clemency must not be given to Penn alone. Barclay and George Whitehead had much to do with it (see sketch of Barclay).

James at once showed Penn marked favour. He would converse with him whilst peers were kept waiting. He told him frankly "he would deal openly with his subjects. He himself was a Catholic, and he desired no peaceable person to be disturbed on account of his opinions; but . . . with the new parliament would rest the power legally to establish liberty of conscience." No way of gaining the king's ear would compare with securing the Friend as advocate. So greatly was he sought that we are told by Gerard Crœse (certainly not a very trustworthy authority) that two hundred applicants sometimes thronged his house at once to secure his interest. We must remember however that Barclay's influence was almost as great. The king was bent on securing the good will of the Quaker leaders. They alone amongst Protestants demanded religious liberty for Catholics; they alone showed them charity. Besides, to shew kindness to the Quakers gave a colour to the king's profession that he was for general toleration, not merely for favour to the Catholics. Whilst James II. was king, therefore, Penn exerted great influence at court. Rightly or wrongly he believed that James and some of his friends, notably the duke of Buckingham, were disposed to labour heartily for liberty of conscience. His friend Barclay had the same confidence as regards the king. It is easy for us to be wise after the event, and to believe that in all this James was scheming for Catholic ascendancy; but that must not prevent our giving Penn credit for good faith. Penn used his utmost influence to strengthen this disposition. In 1686, when on a "religious visit" to Holland, he undertook a commission from the king to the Prince of Orange to induce him to favour a general toleration of religious opinions in England, and the removal of all tests. This commission brought him into collision with Burnett, who was at the same court pleading for toleration but for retaining tests. Their intercourse left such a bitterness in the mind of Burnett that he can never mention Penn but with acrimony.

For this attendance at court he had to pay the penalty of being suspected a Papist. At his very first public discussion with Vincent, the nickname Jesuit had been given him and had stuck to him ever after. The Quakers were many of them branded with the same opprobrious name. In the case of Barclay, there was his early training and boyish conversion to Romanism, and the fact that many of his family were Catholics, to give plausibility to the charge. As to the body at large, "it was believed that the doctrine of the inner light was taught by Jesuit, and that a Franciscan friar had said no churches came so near his own as the Quakers."* The Friends could not accept the ordinary teaching of the

---

* Penn himself writes "There is a people called 'the silent' or 'people of rest' in Italy, at Naples and at Rome itself, that come near Friends; an inward people from all ceremonies and self-worship, [he means worship unprompted and unaided by the Holy Spirit,] seekers, the Pope and two cardinals favour them. A poor Spanish Friar, called Molino, is the first of them. A thousand in Naples it is thought."— DR. STOUGHTON'S LIFE, p. 228.

supremacy of the Bible as a rule of faith, and sometimes on this point their destructive criticism was welcome to Catholics but galling to Protestants. Then they could not take the oath of allegiance and supremacy. So the popular charge was not without some plausible though utterly delusive pretexts.

Now the impression that Penn was a Jesuit at heart, in spite of his Quaker dress and profession, gained ground fast. Tillotson had his fears that the charge was true, and said so; but on Penn assuring him that there was no truth in the charge, he fully and honourably apologised. But for long the suspicion clung to Penn and would not be cast off. That he was determined in all things to keep a clear conscience at all costs is manifest from his conduct in connection with James' efforts to secure Magdalen College, Oxford, for one of his tools. Penn had several times before strained his favour with the king to the last point of endurance, until in one instance the king threatened to turn him out of the room. In this case he wrote a letter so bold and uncompromising as to fill us with amazement. He calls the act one which could not in justice be defended. Such mandates as the king addressed to the fellows he calls a force to conscience and not very agreeable to his other gracious indulgences. Yet because in this matter Penn at first, before he fully understood the case, thought some concessions might be made by the College, Macaulay charges him with simony of the very worst kind. The only other ground for such a charge is the jesting remark of Penn to the deputation that waited on him at Windsor. "If the Bishop of Oxford die, Dr. Hough may be made bishop. What think you of that, gentlemen?" This might have been understood as a hint that, if Dr. Hough would withdraw his opposition, it might be better for him, *if it had not been for Dr. Hough's own words.* But whatever Penn may have said in jest (possibly not wisely) we should remember that

Dr. Hough after the interview thanked God that *he did not hint at a compromise.*

Penn had already used his influence with the king in favour of John Locke. On his return from Holland, he obtained a pardon for "such exiled Presbyterians as were not guilty of treason." One of these was Sir Robert Stuart, of Coltness, who on returning home found his estates in the hands of James, Earl of Arran. The two friends met in London, and Penn congratulated the restored exile. "Ah! Mr. Penn, Arran has got my estate, and I fear my situation is about to be now worse than ever." "What dost thou say?" exclaimed Penn, "thou surprises and grievest me exceedingly. Come to my house to-morrow, and I will set matters right." Penn at once sought the Earl of Arran. "What is this, friend James, that I hear of thee? Thou hast taken possession of Coltness' estate. Thou knowest *that it is not thine.*" The Earl replied, "That estate I paid a great price for. I received no other reward for my expensive and troublesome embassy to France except this estate, and I am certainly much out of pocket by the bargain." "All very well, friend James, but of this assure thyself, that if thou dost not give this moment an order on thy chamberlain for £100 to Coltness, to carry him down to his native country, and £100 to subsist on till matters are adjusted, I will make it as many thousands out of thy way with the king." The earl complied, and after the Revolution Coltness recovered his estate. The earl had to refund all the rents he had received, less by the £300 he had advanced. This may be justice, but it was carried out in rather high-handed fashion.

At the Yearly Meeting in May, 1687, the Quakers at Penn's instance expressed their gratitude to the king for the declaration of liberty of conscience for England which he had issued in the previous month. Mindful however of the strain of royal power by which the relief was obtained, they inserted in the address this significant clause:—"We hope the good effects thereof for the peace, trade, and prosperity of the Kingdom will produce *such a concurrence from the Parliament* as may secure it to our posterity in after times." The King in his reply to the deputation who presented the address, said he hoped before he died to settle it so that after ages shall have no reason to alter it.

Events now rapidly developed the Revolution of 1688. Penn had enjoyed the favour of James, and had felt for him some real regard in spite of his faults. So when William became King, his position was difficult in the extreme. He met the danger with characteristic truthfulness and openness. In his maxims, he says, "Nothing needs a trick, but a trick, sincerity loathes one." So he now acted. He avowed his past relations to the dethroned Monarch. He did not pretend to have changed, but he should accept the result of events, and certainly could not conscientiously plot against the Government. He was several times arrested and examined, but his perfect innocence was always clearly established. It might be proved by an intercepted letter that James had written to him, but he answered that he could not prevent that; it did not prove that he had treasonable designs. William, who had been favourably impressed by him at the Hague, believed his assertions.

In 1689, he had the joy of seeing his labours crowned by the passing of the Act of Toleration. For this he had toiled and suffered, written books and held conferences. Now the end was gained, and his friends and other Dissenters might worship God in peace. Yet strange to say, from this time the number of Quakers so far from increasing, diminished. They had thriven in adversity, in prosperity they declined. But probably one great reason was that quietism overspread the Society, and its aggressive efforts languished. Its members continued faithful to their "testimonies," but became sadly careless about the unconverted around them.

Their grandest evangelist, Fox, was their strongest bulwark against the quietistic spirit. He not only worked indefatigably himself, but was very successful in stirring up and directing others. In 1690, he was called to his rest. Penn hovered around his dying bed, and when all over, he sent the news to Fox's widow in a letter full of warm sympathy and generous appreciation of his leader, or "honourable elder," as Friends preferred to call him. In spite of Fox's very noticeable imperfections, none could appreciate better than Penn his many excellencies and his energetic and noble-spirited labours. Only a few weeks before, Robert Barclay was laid to rest in his own grounds at Ury. As a gentleman and a scholar, no doubt there were points of sympathy between him and Penn which did not link Fox and Penn. But in aggressive energy, in evangelistic labours, and in entire freedom from the taint of quietism, Fox was much more after Penn's own heart than was Barclay. He edited Fox's journal and Barclay's works, supplying each with an elaborate preface.

During the next four years, he was mostly "in retirement" in private lodgings, in London, to avoid the warrants issued against him at the instance of an infamous informer, named Fuller. This man was afterwards denounced by Parliament as a notorious cheat and impostor. Yet, it is evident that he was really dangerous, for one of his victims was actually executed. So Penn deemed it wisest to live in privacy till the storm blew over. But he was far from idle. Besides the work already mentioned, he wrote his famous "Maxims" and other books. Other calamities befel him one after another, until his condition was indeed forlorn. The King deprived him of the government of Pennsylvania. Roguish agents robbed and defrauded him, until neither his colony nor his Irish estates yielded him anything. He was reduced to such straits, that when once he thought of going to Pennsylvania he had not the means. Friends looked coldly on him, in spite of his pathetic appeal to them not to forsake him in his hour of need. To fill up the bitter cup, in 1693 he lost his wife, the joy and consolation of his days of trial, the constant, indefatigable, and undaunted sharer of his labours. He had the melancholy knowledge that her end was hastened by her taking to heart her husband's crushing cares and unmerited ill-usage.

The coolness of the Quakers needs explanation. There was then, as now, a strong feeling amongst some religious people against Christian men taking an active part in public affairs. Penn was too strong a man to yield to it, but it caused him much trouble and suffering. And now that William reigned, and that Penn's position, instead of being a help and a protection to Friends, caused them to be suspected of disloyalty, this feeling was intensified. George Fox's son-in-law, Thomas Lower, even sketched a form of apology, which Penn was to sign to satisfy the weaker brethren. Penn once joined some Friends in Pennsylvania when they had given him up, supposing that opposing winds and tide made his coming impossible. When they expressed their astonishment at seeing him under the circumstances, he answered with that ready pleasantry which ever characterised him, "I have been sailing against wind and tide all my life."

But, with sublime Christian heroism, he accepted his lot. He strengthened himself by much waiting on God, and by such intercourse with the best spirits around him as circumstances permitted. In his Maxims we have not only whatever of his own prudence could be crystallised; we have also clear evidence of his own habit of looking at earthly things in heavenly light, and of endeavouring to discover their spiritual meaning and use.

At last, in God's mercy, the tide turned. The night had been very dark, but the tardy dawn came at length, and ushered in a bright though not a cloudless day.

Cruelly deserted by the colonists, for whom he had done and suffered so much, he found gratitude amongst "worldly" statesmen and courtiers. The Earl of Rochester, Lord Somers, and others took the case in hand. He asked them to gain him a full and public hearing before the King and Council. His defence was completely successful. The charges against him were quashed. It was proved that he had done nothing to forfeit his patent, and was restored to his government and proprietary. This consolation came to him at a time when it was greatly needed. He had lost his wife, and now his favorite son, Springett, was slowly dying of consumption.

We must not pass by the death of his wife so briefly. No doubt, the sad event was hastened by her wifely sympathy with her husband in his great troubles. Yet she had the happiness of seeing the bulk of them removed before she died. "She quietly expired," says Penn, "in my arms, her head upon my bosom, with a sensible and devout resignation of her soul to Almighty God. I hope I may say she was a public as well as private loss, for she was not only an excellent wife and mother, but an entire and constant friend, of a more than common capacity, and greater modesty and humility, yet most equal and undaunted in danger." Their wedded life had been a beautiful blending of romantic passion with sober Christian usefulness. Religion, and culture, and practical philanthropy had gone hand-in-hand in their social life.

Whilst speaking of this bitter cross, it will be well to anticipate a little, and record the death of his favorite son, Springett. This noble and gifted youth died of consumption. Penn did all that a father's love could suggest, all that personal attention could do to lengthen his days. But the end, though slow in its approach, was yet too sure, and the darling boy expired in his father's arms early in 1696.

The younger son, William, was of a very different stamp. Cavalier grace, and sensuousness which degenerated into sensuality, marked his character. Martial and generous in disposition, with no mean capacity for business, he early shewed a tendency to idle frivolousness and then to gross indulgence, which caused his father the keenest pain. The refined enjoyments of his home were not to his taste, so he sought in foreign cities the worst indulgences they could afford. And when his father was far away in Pennsylvania, he launched out into riot and excesses which filled that father's heart with shame and dismay.

Early in 1696, William Penn married as his second wife Hannah Callowhill of Bristol, a woman of great energy and ability. She was an admirable helper in all good works.

For six years after his restoration to his rights, Penn was content to leave Pennsylvania in the hands of his cousin, Colonel Markham. His principal employments then were literary and ministerial.

In 1694, we find him using his new-found liberty to preach in the West of England. His standing in the Society of Friends had been re-assured; the usual certificate given by the brethren to all their preachers who travel, stating that he was a "minister in unity and good esteem among us," could be freely given, and he visited his brethren with comfort and acceptance. He travelled, therefore, in the Western counties, "having meetings almost daily in the most considerable towns and other places in those counties, to which the people flocked abundantly; and his testimony to the truth answering to that of God in their consciences was assented to by many." We are told that the Mayors of these towns generally consented to their having the Town Halls for their meetings, "for the respect they had for him, few places else being sufficient to hold the meetings." Returning to London, he had a more painful duty to perform, which the following extract from a contemporary letter describes.

Henry Goulding, of London, to Robert Barclay, junr., 28th of 12th mo., 1694.

"Being now a writing, I think it not unfit to acquaint thee in a brief hint what passed at Ratcliff meeting, last First-day (Sunday) week, where was William Penn, John Vaughton, and George Keith. The latter having had no time till the breaking up of the meeting, he then desired to be heard. Friends all stayed. After a short appologie, he fell a reflecting on the manner of John Vaughton's going to prayer, calling it a hasty sacrifice, comparing to Saul's. Then he fell upon doctrinall points, reflecting on our unsoundness, particularly the epistle of John i. 7; saying that the blood there mentioned was by us preacht only misticall, whereas, he affirmed, it had no such signification, neither did any there say to the contrary. In short, the tendency of all he said was to expose Friends as unsound. 'Twas a great and mixt meeting. William Penn grew uneasy; after about a quarter-of-an-hour, he stood up, saying to this purpose, 'In the name of the Lord, he was concerned to sound the truth over the head of this apostate and common opposer.' After a few words, George Keith was silent. William Penn opened to the people our belief of the virtue and efficacy of the blessed blood shed on the Cross; and also shewed the people the reason why we did not so frequently press Christ's death and sufferings as in the Apostles' days, they being concerned among such as believed not his outward coming, but among Christiandom was the notion generally held, but that of the inward denied and opposed. When he had done, George Keith would be speaking, but Friends went away, and left him in a great anger and quarrell."

In Barclay's "Inner Life, &c.," it is rightly said that Keith's expulsion was not for unsound doctrine, though he charged the brethren with being unsound, but for contempt of authority. He tried to gather a congregation in London, but his following seems to have very soon dwindled, for a letter to Robert Barclay, junr., dated London, 22nd of December, 1696, after speaking of the fierce counterfires of pamphlets concerning his controversy, says "Last Fifth-day (Thursday) George Keith had but 10 or 12 at his meeting. His show is much over. But his enmity remains. Oh, that he might see his declension, and repent of the evil he hath done, if it be the Lord's will."

George Keith had been Penn's fellow-labourer and fellow-sufferer. To see him now attacking his old friends, and manifesting such a bitter and factious spirit, was most painful. In 1696, after Keith was disowned by the Society Penn endeavoured to neutralize the effect of his misrepresentations by a work entitled "More work for George Keith." In this, he reproduces from Keith's former publications abundant replies to his present statements. There is ample proof that, as in Naylor's case, Friends clung lovingly to the misguided man to the very last.* [For his after confession of his fault see sketch of Barclay.]

---

* To this period belongs also the following letter, inserted as a specimen of Penn's familiar correspondence with his brethren. The three or four months service, to which he refers, is the journey in the West, already spoken of.

W. Penn to R. B., junr.

London, the 7th of the 12th mo., 1694.

Dear and well-beloved Friend,

My heart is much affected with the Lord's goodness to thee and thy dear relations, that he has remembered you, among the many in Israel, whom this day he is visiting with his loving power and spring of life, so that they had have sitten dry and barren, are now blossoming as a rose and bringing forth to the praises of Him that has called them. Wherefore, dear Robert, let thine eye be above the world and the comforts that fade, to the unfading glory, and keep close to the Lord, that thou mayest come through openings and visions to possessions, and like a good souldier encounter the enemy in his appearances as well to ensnare by the lawful as the unlawful things; and approve thy heart to the Lord in the way of the Cross and daily dying and living. O! great is the mystery of godliness, but the grace is sufficient! I rejoice at Peter Gardiner's good service; the Lord will

It has ever been a custom of the Quakers to seek the presence of the great and the powerful, not for personal advantages, but in order to urge on them the claims of religion, and the opportunities and responsibilities of their position. In many instances, the results of these interviews speak for themselves, but as they justly hold, duty does not depend on results. In such a spirit, William Penn sought Peter the Great, in 1696, when he was working as a shipwright, at Greenwich. The young Czar asked many questions about the Friends and their views. It is amusing to find him asking Thomas Story of what use would they be to any kingdom if they would not fight. That he was more than amused by the peculiar views and manners of the Friends, is evident from his remark after a sermon preached by a Friend in Denmark, that whoever could live according to such doctrines, would be happy.

Penn made a second, and as it proved, a final voyage to America, in 1699. He intended to settle there with his wife and family, and made his arrangements accordingly. But events were too strong for him, and he returned in about two years, and never again crossed the Atlantic. It is certain, however, that even after this, he intended to return and spend the rest of his days in the colony. In a letter written three years afterwards, he said, "Had you settled a reasonable revenue, I would have returned and laid my bones among you, and my wife's, too, after her mother's death."

Yet, in this short time, he had done much for Pennsylvania. Bills against piracy and smuggling, and for

---

work when, how, and by whom He will. I have had three or four months sore travel with blessed success; blessed be His Name. . . Dear Robert, in the love of the precious truth, in which I desire thou maist grow up to fill thy dear and honorable father's place, I bid thee farewell. I am,

Thy reall and affectionate friend,
WILLIAM PENN.

P. S.—My journey for Ireland will not be soon, as I hoped, but shall inform thee. Vale.

the just treatment of negroes, had been passed; better arrangements for the health and improvement of Philadelphia had been made, and a new Charter or frame of Government, and a just system of taxation had been introduced, the expense of governing the Province having, hitherto, fallen on the Governor. Even now, no provision was made for his claims as proprietor. Treaties were made with the Susquehannah and other tribes of Indians; and finally, just on the eve of the Governor's departure, Philadelphia was incorporated. Many minor acts were passed, some of them curiously illustrating the colonists' ideas of a paternal and religious government. Not only were sins against purity and honesty to be punished, but, amongst others, bills were passed on the following matters: the spreading of false news, the names of the days and months of the year, to prevent cursing and swearing, against scolding, for the dimensions of casks, and true packing of meat, against drunkenness and drinking healths, and against selling rum to the Indians. This much was accomplished by the Assembly; probably, more would have been done, but for abounding jealousies. The Province and the other Territories (the districts purchased from the Duke of York) were jealous of each other, and both were jealous of the Governor.

In July, 1701, Penn received a communication from the king, which sorely puzzled him. It demanded that the American proprietaries should unite for the defence of the Colonies, and that Pennsylvania should contribute £350 for the defence of the New York frontier. Apostle of peace though he was, he could do no otherwise than lay the letter before the Assembly. That body delayed and finessed, and finally, saying nothing of peace principles, pleaded their poverty as a reason for postponing the further consideration of the matter, until it was more urgent. Thus, this question of peace, which so long divided Pennsylvania, was for the present shelved. But it is the boast of Friends that for 70 years Pennsylvania had no army, and though so near both Indians and Frenchmen, suffered nothing through the lack of one. That State "subsisted in the midst of six Indian nations," says Oldmixon, "without so much as a militia for her defence. Whatever the quarrels of the Pennsylvanian Indians were with others, they uniformly respected and held as it were sacred, the territories of William Penn. The Pennsylvanians never lost man, woman, or child by them, which neither the colony of Maryland, nor that of Virginia could say, no more than the great colony of New England." To complete the argument for non-resistance, see what occurred when Pennsylvania got an army. "From that hour the Pennsylvanians transferred their confidence in Christian principles to a confidence in their arms; and from that hour to the present they have been subject to war." (Dymond's Essays, 4th edition, p. 192.)

But it must not be supposed that the refusal to fight meant either unwillingness or inability to use moral means for self-protection. In 1701, Penn heard of a riot in East Jersey, and set off at once with some friends to quell it. It was put down before he reached the spot, but gave him occasion fully to state his views. "If lenitives would not do, coercives should be tried. The leaders should be eyed, and some should be forced to declare them by the rigour of the law; and those who were found to be such should bear the burden of such sedition, which would be the best way to behead the body without danger."

Amidst all this care and work, Penn found time to make preaching tours in Pennsylvania, New Jersey and Maryland. He and his family won a warm place in the hearts of the Friends here, as well as elsewhere. He might have a large and handsome house at Pennsbury, and his style of living might be superior to that of his neighbours; but he could pick up a bare-legged Quaker girl and give her a ride behind him to "meeting," and he had a kindly word and pleasantry for the poor as much as for the rich. "The Governor is our pater patriæ," writes one of the Colonists, "and his worth is no new thing to us. His excellent wife is beloved of all."

As Pennsylvania was the birthplace of Abolition, the German Friends at Germantown first raising the question, it is interesting to see what Penn did in the matter. He passed a Bill for regulating the trial and punishment of negro wrong-doers. But he wished to go further, and proposed that negro marriages should be legal, and that the rights of negro-women should be secured by law; but the Assembly threw out these Bills. In 1696 the Philadelphia Yearly Meeting had resolved that buying, selling, and holding slaves was contrary to the teachings of Christianity. Penn followed up this resolution by urging on the Society of Friends in Pennsylvania the recognition of the spiritual claims of negroes. Henceforth, until the Society insisted on its members liberating their slaves, they were taught the Scriptures, and encouraged to attend divine worship.

Penn arrived at Portsmouth, in the middle of December, 1701, after a voyage of about six weeks. The chief business that called him home, was the scheme of William III. for amalgamating all the American provinces as regal Governments. To his intense relief, that scheme was dropped. Soon after this, the king died, and Queen Anne, the daughter of Penn's friend and guardian, James II., ascended the throne. He once more enjoyed royal favour in a marked degree. He was chosen to present to the Queen the Quaker address, thanking her for promising to maintain the Act of Toleration. After the address was read, "Mr. Penn," said the Queen, "I am so well pleased that what I have said is to your satisfaction, that you and your Friends may be assured of my protection."

Of the remaining years of Penn's life, we have very imperfect accounts. He edited the works of two Quaker ministers, those of John Whitehead in 1704; those of John Banks, in 1711. In 1709, he wrote "Some account of the Life and Writings of Bulstrode Whitlocke, Esq.," the famous lawyer and stout Puritan, whom he had known and greatly esteemed. He also travelled repeatedly as a minister, and took an active interest in the affairs of the Quakers. Thus, in 1710, Sir D. Dalrymple writes to R. Barclay, junr., who had written to him about the sufferings of Edinboro' Friends:—"I have written fully to Mr. Penn by this post, who had written to me upon the same subject, to whom I refer you." Again, in 1711, he with others waited on the Duke of Ormond (whom he had known before he became a Friend) to thank him for the kindness which he had shewn to Friends in Ireland during his Lord Lieutenancy.

Meantime had occurred the sad troubles with his late agent Philip Ford, which crippled his resources, broke down his health, and even at one time made him a prisoner in the Fleet for debt. Oldmixon states the fact thus:—"The troubles that befel Mr. Penn in the latter part of his life are of a nature too private to have a place in a public history. He trusted an ungrateful, unjust agent too much with the management of it; and when he expected to have been thousands of pounds the better, found himself thousands of pounds in debt: insomuch that he was restrained in his liberty within the privilege of the Fleet by a tedious and unsuccessful law suit, which together with age, broke his spirits, not easy to be broken, and rendered himself incapable of business and society, as he was wont to have been in the days of his health and vigour both of body and mind." The story is a very sad one. Ford was a Quaker lawyer, and undoubtedly Penn had been far too trustful and careless with him. He had even borrowed money from him on the security of his colony. Ford repaid his kindness and trust by cheating him out of thousands, and his widow and son went farther, and tried to snatch the colony from Penn's grasp. But it was ruled that "it would not be decent to make Government ambulatory," and their claim was not allowed.

The trouble thus caused resulted in Penn having several apoplectic fits, which left him thoroughly shattered. For six years he lingered in second childhood, lovingly nursed by his wife. The best account of his last days occurs in the Journal of Thomas Story, a distinguished Quaker minister, a scholar and a naturalist, whom he had made the first recorder of Philadelphia.

The end came very gently and peacefully. After the long and stormy voyage, the vessel came into harbour through unwonted calms and waters almost without a ripple. He was laid in his grave in Jordan's meeting-house beside his dearly loved Guli, and not far from his mother and Isaac Pennington. Many gathered there to pay the last honours. And since that day, the spot hallowed by his dust has been a well-visited shrine, where many have not only thought admiringly of his deeds, but have also thanked God for the grace that was in him.

If Macaulay was prejudiced against Penn, his testimony to his world-wide fame is the more reliable. We will quote it as it stands. "Rival nations and hostile sects have agreed in canonising him. England is proud of his name. A great commonwealth beyond the Atlantic regards him with a reverence similar to that which the Athenians felt for Theseus, and the Romans for Quirinus. The respected society of which he was a member honours him as an apostle. By pious men of other denominations he is usually regarded as a bright pattern of Christian virtue. Meanwhile admirers of a very different sort have sounded his praises. The French philosophers of the eighteenth century pardoned what they regarded as his superstitious fancies in consideration of his contempt for priests, and of his cosmopolitan benevolence, impartially extended to all races and to all creeds. His name has thus become, throughout all civilised countries, a synonym for probity and philanthropy."

"Nor is this reputation altogether unmerited. Penn was without doubt a man of eminent virtues. He had a strong sense of religious duty, and a fervent desire to promote the happiness of mankind. On one or two points of high importance he had notions more correct than were in his day common, even among men of enlarged minds; and as the proprietor and legislator of a province, which, being almost uninhabited when it came into his possession, afforded a clear field for moral experiments, he had the rare good fortune of being able to carry his theories into practice without any compromise, and yet without any shock to existing institutions. He will always be mentioned with honour as the founder of a Colony, who did not in his dealings with a savage people abuse the strength derived from civilisation, and as a law-giver who in an age of persecution, made religious liberty the corner-stone of a polity."

This testimony is bare justice, indeed it needs supplementing. Macaulay has done justice to his fame, but not to his usefulness or to his beautiful character. For to use the beautiful figure which the Rt. Hon. W. E. Forster employs, "like as the citizens of Philadelphia are even now building the streets which he planned on the unpeopled waste, so are the workmen in the temple of freedom yet labouring at the design which he sketched out." And in the work they have not only his designs to assist them, but the inspiration of his noble life to stimulate them.

The story of Penn's life, so noble and yet so sad in many parts, has touched many hearts. "He reminds me of Abraham or Æneas more than any one else," says Professor Seeley. "I find him," says Tennyson, (writing

Mar. 3rd, 1882, to the Historical Society of Pennsylvania), no comet of a season, but the fixed light of a dark and graceless age, shining into the present—a good man and true." In Caroline Fox's "Memories of Old Friends" we read,—"He (Ernest de Bunsen) has been translating William Penn's life into German and sent a copy to Humboldt, from whom he received two charming letters about it, in one saying that he has read every word, and that the contemplation of such a life has contributed to the peace of his old age."

Such testimonies could be multiplied indefinitely. The character and life that inspire such feelings need no defence and no eulogy.

ROBERT BARCLAY,

THE

APOLOGIST OF QUAKERISM.

PREFACE.

This sketch was outlined as a companion sketch to those of Fox and Penn. But the opportunity of embodying in it extracts from unpublished letters in the keeping of members of the Barclay family, (for which the author cannot be too grateful,) led to its being enlarged to a disproportionate size. But the reader will not regret this, when he finds himself furnished with new materials throwing light on a character so little understood. To most readers, Barclay is merely a name; the author has attempted to realise the man and his work, as far as the still very imperfect information will allow.

ROBERT BARCLAY,

THE

APOLOGIST OF QUAKERISM.

GEORGE FOX, that fervid evangelist who anticipated Wesley in claiming the whole world as his parish, visited Scotland only once. This was in 1657. But some years previously, several Quaker ministers, including two lady-evangelists, Catherine Evans and Sarah Cheevers, had preached "the truth" there, and meetings had been gathered, says Sewel the Quaker historian, in Edinburgh, Aberdeen, and other places. James Naylor preached in Scotland as early as 1651, with his usual fervour and success. But no church of professed "Friends" was formed in Aberdeen until 1662, when Alexander Jaffray sometime provost of Aberdeen, one of the Scottish Commissioners to King Charles, and a member of Cromwell's Parliament, was led along with others to a full and open acceptance of Quakerism by William Dewsbury. The number of the names was small, but they were men and women whose energy and sterling worth made them noteworthy. Their decision may be measured by their daring the contempt so profusely accorded the "Friends" by the orthodox; "possessed with the devil, demented, blasphemous deniers of the true Christ" being some of the expressions hurled at them by the neighbouring pulpits. In 1666, they were strengthened by the accession of Colonel David Barclay, and a little later by that of his son, Robert Barclay, the future Apologist of Quakerism. Fully then was the expectation of George Fox realised, of which he afterwards told Robert Barclay, in 1675, "As soon as ever my horse set his foot upon the land of the Scottish nation, the infinite sparkles of life sparkled about me; and so as I rid with divers friends, I saw the seed of the seedsman Christ that was sown; but abundance of clods—foul and filthy earth—was above it; and a great winter and storms and tempests of work." "Thick cloddy earth of hypocrisy and falseness atop," says the corresponding passage of his journal, "and a briary brambly nature, which is to be turned up with God's Word, and ploughed up with his spiritual plough, before God's seed brings forth heavenly and spiritual fruit to his glory. But the husbandman is to wait in patience."

David Barclay represented an ancient and honourable family, supposed to be a branch of the Berkeleys in Gloucestershire. He was a lineal descendant of Theobald de Berkeley, born about 1110, who held a large estate in Kincardine, and was conspicuous in the court of David I. In the 15th century, Alexander Berkeley began to spell the name Barclay, and his descendants followed his example.* They were a powerful, sometimes a turbulent race, with an occasional instance of a literary or scholarly scion. David Barclay's father having wrecked his fortune by spendthrift and easy-going habits, his sons had to shift for themselves. Three of them died before their father, two in infancy, the third, James, falling at the battle of Philiphaugh, whilst fighting under his brother David. Of the two survivors, the younger, Robert, became a Catholic priest, and flourished in Paris, becoming Rector of the Scottish College there. Of David, the elder and the father of the subject of this sketch, we must speak more at length.

---

* Of the father of this Alexander de Barclay, whose name was David, we read that he was the "ringleader of the savage barons who exaggerated the atrocities of a reckless age by actually boiling an obnoxious sheriff of the Mearns in a cauldron, and then 'suppin' the broo'." Yet the son was something of a poet, and some lines full of good advice, said to be from his pen, are given in the "Short Account of R. Barclay."

David Barclay was born at Kirtounhill, in 1610. The only patrimony he got from his father was a good education: for in 1633, the old family estates were sold to pay off his father's debts. Finding that he had to make his own way in the world, with all the energy of his race he "flung himself into the saddle of opportunity as a soldier of fortune," and rose to the rank of major in the army of Gustavus Adolphus, specially distinguishing himself at Lutzen. Returning home with substantial gains as well as honours, when the civil war broke out he became a colonel in the Royal Army. He fought under Leslie at Philiphaugh, and effectively assisted Middleton in holding the north, until Cromwell removed him from command, after his victory at Preston-pans. Then he retired from military service, bought the Ury estate, and with his wife and son Robert settled there. He had contracted an advantageous marriage in the spring of 1648, with Catherine, daughter of Sir Robert Gordon, of Gordonstown. The father was the second son of the Earl of Sutherland and second cousin to James I. He was a man of great parts, and held various high offices under the Crown. After his marriage, David Barclay sat in Parliament for Sutherland, and then for Angus and Kincardine. He used his influence to regain possession of his Ury estate which had been seized by General Monk, and to befriend other gentlemen who were in similar trouble, and his success in these efforts made him very popular. Then he retired into private life. In 1663, he lost his excellent wife when Robert was not fifteen. But before her death, she took one step of the greatest moment to Robert. He had been sent to Paris, to finish his education under his uncle's eye. But though his progress must have satisfied even a mother's pride, she, herself a staunch Protestant, felt a great anxiety lest he should adopt the Romish faith. So, when dying of consumption, she obtained from his father the promise that he should be recalled home.

This step was farther urged by her mother, good old lady Gordon, in an earnest letter which still exists. Accordingly Col. Barclay visited his brother in Paris in 1664, and after vigorous opposition from him, brought his son home.

But the time had come for a complete change in the tone and tenour of David Barclay's life. He had gained renown and position, and had allied himself with a branch of the Royal family, but these had brought him neither peace nor satisfaction. Royal blood is no guarantee against disease and death, and he had had to see his beloved wife fade away and die at the early age of forty-three. He had risked limb and life, and had striven with hand and brain to win renown, and position, and wealth, only to find that these things expose their possessor to special trials and dangers. He had found out by hard experience how uncertain was his tenure of earthly good. His sorrows and disappointments prepared his heart for more earnestness about spiritual truth than he had hitherto manifested, and Quakerism was to present that truth in a form which would satisfy his mind and heart.

Perhaps it was whilst on the journey to fetch home his son, that he became closely acquainted with the Quakers. He tells us how he had heard of their simple and conscientious living, and " he considered within himself that if they were really such as even their enemies were forced to acknowledge, there must be something extraordinary about them." Whether or not this knowledge was gained in Aberdeen, where a meeting had been gathered now more than a year, we do not know. But, "being in London" on some errand or other, he had opportunities to enquire into the Quaker principles and practises, which he did to such purpose, that his mind became convinced that their tenets were according to the Scriptures. Still, the cautious Scotchman did not immediately join them.

Immediately afterwards we find David Barclay in prison in Edinbro' Castle. Although he had suffered for the king, he was accused of having held office under Cromwell, and it might have gone hardly with him had he not been befriended by his old chief, the Earl of Middleton. Through the influence of that nobleman the proceedings were quashed, and he was liberated.

This imprisonment, in the ordering of God's providence, brought to the right issue the great crisis of his life. In the same room with him in Edinbro' Castle was imprisoned Sir John Swintoune, who from a soldier and a Presbyterian had become a thorough Quaker. He was so zealous in propagating his opinions that the only way to silence him was to keep him in solitary confinement, which was at one time done for several weeks. No wonder, then, that he urged on David Barclay the full acceptance of the truth.

On leaving the Castle, the colonel seems to have remained in Edinbro' even after he had sent his son, in company with a Quaker, David Falconer, to Ury. In Edinbro' he came out as an acknowledged Friend.

He tells us what points satisfied his sober and careful judgment that the Quakers were right. He was struck with the correspondence between their peace principles and Isaiah's prophecy, that in Gospel times they would beat their swords into ploughshares, and their spears into pruning-hooks. Then again, they were all as brothers, loving and standing by each other, and had not Christ said, that his disciples should be known by their mutual love? The courageous soldier was in sympathy with those who, whilst others worshipped God by stealth, bravely dared all persecution by openly assembling to worship God as their consciences dictated. So he thought within himself, that "if the Lord Jesus Christ had a visible Church on earth these must be they." But all this merely cleared the ground for the final and decisive proof, without which he would never have made a Friend. Feeling his judgment satisfied by these tests, he yielded his heart to the influence of the truth, and he experienced a peace which insults and sufferings could not disturb, and gained an experimental acquaintance with God that satisfied the cravings of his soul.

He became distinguished for his solemn fervour in prayer, his deep piety and uncomplaining meekness in ill-usage—the latter, "a virtue," says one of his descendants, "he was before very much unacquainted with." "One of his relations, upon an occasion of uncommon rudeness, lamenting that he should be now treated so differently from what formerly he had been, he answered, that he found more satisfaction as well as honour in being thus insulted for his religious principles, than when, some years before, it was usual for the magistrates as he passed through Aberdeen, to meet him several miles, and conduct him to a public entertainment in their town-house, and then convey him so far out again, in order to gain his favour." This noble testimony is the subject of one of Whittier's most spirited ballads. The old soldier lived to a ripe old age, his son only surviving him four years.

We have thus traced the career of the father, that we may better understand the influences through which the son passed before his hearty acceptance of Quakerism. He belonged to a family divided in religious opinions, some of the Catholic faith, some Protestant to the core. His abilities, connections, and worldly expectations, all invited him to a distinguished career. Yet from the noblest and purest motives he turned away from brilliant prospects, and from older and more respected churches, and linked himself with a new, despised and persecuted sect.

Robert Barclay was born at Gordonstown, Oct. 23rd, 1648. From both sides of his parentage, he seems to have inherited scholarly ability and literary tastes. His grandfather, Sir Robert Gordon, was a man of culture and refinement, and his great-grandfather, John Gordon (father-in-law of Sir Robert), was Dean of Sarum, a good classical scholar and a keen theologian. On the other side, the Barclays seem to have supplied the Catholic church with several theologians and scholars. From early years he gave promise of great intellectual powers, which were sedulously cultivated at the best schools that Scotland possessed. His uncle Robert offered to look after his education, and took him in hand, as he tells us, when he had "scarcely got out of his childhood." But early as he left Scotland for Paris, he carried with him such impressions of the narrowness and bigotry of his Calvinistic countrymen as remained with him through life. In Paris, his uncle and others so skilfully assailed his Protestant instincts that they succumbed, and he became an avowed Catholic. He was a great favourite with his uncle, who purposed making him his heir, and who watched him through his brilliant college course with the greatest delight.

But whilst his uncle was thus satisfied, his mother's heart was filled with dismay at the thought of her son growing up a Catholic—a consummation for which his scholarly proficiency was poor compensation. She therefore on her death-bed obtained from his father a promise that her son should be brought home.

On this errand the Colonel went to Paris, in 1664. But he found his brother stoutly opposed to parting with his nephew. He met the argument of worldly welfare by offering to buy Robert a larger estate than his father's, and put him in possession immediately. But the boy had a noble reverence for his father in spite of his long absence from home, and his wish settled the question with him, and he replied to all pleas, "He is my father and must be obeyed." So father and son returned home together, and the uncle's property eventually enriched the College of which he was Rector, and other religious houses in France.

When David Barclay was passing through that crisis in his spiritual history which resulted in his embracing Quakerism, he made no efforts to win his son to the same view. No doubt he had all a new convert's confidence in the power of "the truth." Probably he had also a Quaker's persuasion that though such efforts might sway the understanding, they could not "reach" the soul. He said he wished the change to come from conviction, not from imitation.' The early Friends never considered themselves a sect, and did not seek proselytes so much as they sought to spread deep spiritual life. In the end at least, the laissez-faire method resulted in what the father wished. The son quietly looked around on the different classes of professed Christians. He felt his old repugnance to the Calvinists invincible. The latitudinarians, with all their professed charity and condemnation of "judging," pleased him no better. Finally, he gave his hearty allegiance to Friends within twelve months of his father's admission to their fellowship.

It is an interesting question, "What led such a clear and powerful mind to accept Quakerism?"

It could not fail to impress such a nature to see the great change which had passed over his father. The warrior and the man of the world had become a consistent Friend, trusting God to plead his cause, anxious most about spiritual wealth, careful most to walk closely and humbly with God. Further, it seemed to him that whilst others were wonderfully strict in creed, the Friends, whom they called heretics, far surpassed them in holy and exemplary living. Lastly, came the evidence that so often in those days turned the scale decisively in favor of the new brotherhood. The very first time that Robert Barclay attended a Friends' meeting he was struck by the awful Presence there; he felt that God was in that place. Some minister who was present used these epigrammatic words, which are said to have made a great impression on him. "In stilness there is fulness, in fulness there is nothingness, in nothingness there are all things." It is true that we are told that Sir John Swintoune and another Friend named Halliday were specially helpful to him at this critical time. But we have the clearest evidence that what most impressed him and attracted him to Friends was not their ministry, but the marvellous divine influence enjoyed in the period of silent waiting upon God. His intimate friend, Andrew Jaffray, bears testimony that he was "reached" in the time of silence. His own words, too, in his apology are unmistakable; they are introduced into his glowing description of an ideal Friends' meeting, as a personal testimony to the value of silent worship. Speaking of his own conversion, he says, "Who not by strength of argument, or by a particular disquisition of each doctrine, and convincement of my understanding thereby, came to receive and bear witness to the truth, but by being secretly reached by this Life. For when I came into the silent assemblies of God's people, I felt a secret power amongst them which touched my heart; and as I gave way unto it, I found the evil weakening in me, and the good raised up; and so I became thus knit and united unto them, hungering more and more after the increase of this power and life, whereby I might find myself perfectly redeemed." Apology, Prop. XI., Sect. 7.

Boy as Barclay was when he returned from Paris, in spite of his precocity it may be questioned whether his surrender of Catholicism cost him much conflict of soul, though he assures us in his "Vindication," he did "turn from that way not without sincere and real convictions of the errors of it." But beyond question, it would cost him a severe struggle to surrender his proud vantage ground as a scholar, and to join a sect who taught not only that learning was not necessary to a saving knowledge of Christ, but also that it had small share in the efficient ministry of the Gospel. The battle was first fought out in his own search for peace and light. From his childhood he had been ambitious of scholarship. Conscious, as he tells us in the introduction to his treatise on "Universal Love," of abilities beyond the average, he had a pleasure in intellectual pursuits which led him to follow them up with keen relish for their own sakes. But now the appetite was to receive a check, not only that it might ever afterwards keep its right place, but that he might learn how much more effectively God can teach than can the best of men. George Fox had to learn from sad experience that even enlightened Christians cannot stand instead of God. Robert Barclay had to learn by a shorter, but no doubt sharp experience, that his favourite books could do nothing for him in spiritual religion without Christ, and that in spiritual power and spiritual discernment illiterate men might be by far his superiors. He has described the experience in his Apology, when speaking of the insufficiency of learning to make a true minister, and the possibility of being a true minister without it.

"And if in any age since the Apostles' days, God hath purposed to show his power in weak instruments, for the battering down of the carnal and heathenish wisdom, and restoring again the ancient simplicity of truth, this is it. For in our day, God hath raised up witnesses for himself as he did the fishermen of old, many, yea most of whom are labouring and mechanic men, who, altogether without that learning, have by the power and spirit of God, struck at the very root and ground of Babylon; and in the strength and might of this power have gathered thousands by reaching their consciences into the same power and life, who, as to the outward part, have been far more knowing than they, yet not able to resist the virtue that proceeded from them. Of which I myself am a true witness, and can declare from certain experience; because my heart hath often been greatly broken and tendered by that virtuous life that proceeded from the powerful ministry of those illiterate men. . . . What shall I say then to you who are lovers of learning and admirers of knowledge? Was not I also a lover and admirer of it, who also sought after it according to my age and capacity. But it pleased God in his unutterable love, early to withstand my vain endeavours, while I was yet but eighteen years of age, and made me seriously to consider (which I wish may also befal others) that without holiness and regeneration no man can see God; and that the fear of the Lord is the beginning of wisdom, and to depart from iniquity a good understanding; and how much knowledge puffeth up, and leadeth away from that quietness, stillness and humility of mind, where the Lord appears and his heavenly wisdom is revealed. . . . Therefore, seeing that among them (these excellent, though despised, because illiterate witnesses of God) I with many others, have found the heavenly food that gives contentment, let my soul seek after this learning, and wait for it for ever." Truth Triumphant, p. 426.

In the means and mode of his conversion Robert Barclay was like many of his co-religionists in Scotland. It is an interesting feature of Scottish Quakerism that a number of its adherents were not gained by preaching. Many of the early Friends tell us that they adopted the Quaker views before they knew of the existence of any society which held such views. Their hearts yearned after an ideal which they did not find in any existing sect. But when Quakerism was presented to their view, they recognised in it the features which they had learned to love. The case of Alexander Jaffray is fairly representative of others, and his diary enables us to watch the process in minute detail in most of its stages. The awakened soul gets disgusted with chopping logic, and with manipulating the dry bones of a formal theology. It longs for bread and is offered a stone. It longs for pure spiritual life and for true holiness, and for an experimental acquaintance with God that shall satisfy its quickened instincts; and instead it finds the sects around it mostly busied with preparations for living rather than with life, ever constructing scientific scaffolding but not building, keenly discussing the right attitude of the soul towards God rather than having actual dealings with Him. Quakerism comes on the scene and at once commends itself to such a soul by dealing with the practical life, putting the teaching and promises of the Bible to the test of experience, and finding that they actually work and lead to assured conviction, hearty consecration, and holy living. Modern Quakerism has come to be associated with a few negations; primitive Quakerism won its triumphs by a robust and full-blooded spiritual life. The Assembly's catechism correctly defined the chief end of man to be "to glorify God and to enjoy Him forever." The Friends exemplified the definition in actual life. Most professing Christians, in spite of their beautifully finished creed, were still in bondage to questions like these: "Shall we succeed in life, and what will men think of us, and how will they treat us, if we act up to our convictions?" Such questions troubled the Quakers very little. They acted as if they believed religion a sufficient end and object in life, worth living for, and worth dying for. This was the way in which they glorified God, and so they did enjoy Him even in this life. They had great peace and joy in believing. The power of God was in their gatherings and attended their ministry. They were mighty in prayer, and did wonders through their strong faith. Their acquaintance with experimental religion was astonishing, and their knowledge of the word of God extensive and practically useful, such as might be expected from men who searched it lovingly, and relied upon its counsels in the affairs of life. Above all they were enabled to do what they most aspired to do, to live a holy life. They were rich not only in gifts but in grace. All this commended Quakerism to such men as Swintoune and Jaffray and the Barclays. It was better proof than the exactest syllogism, and far more satisfying to the soul than the best compacted creed.

Henceforth Robert Barclay's life is closely connected with the history of Quakerism, and especially of Quakerism in northern Scotland. He did not travel so much as many Friends beyond his own country in the service of the gospel, but his position, wealth, and learning were freely devoted to the service of "the truth." It is not clear that the same earnest evangelising spirit prevailed in Scotland which inspired the English Friends. For some reason the society never gained such numbers north of the Tweed as it did in England. Possibly they were too jealous of activity. In a letter of Christian Barclay's, written after her husband's death, I find a sad instance of that mischievous overvaluing of silence, which did so much harm amongst the Quakers in the eighteenth century. Writing to Friends in and about Aberdeen, she says, after a warning against "needless jesting,"—"in the bowels of motherly love is my heart towards you all, desiring we may all travel more and more into silence, for it is a safe place. Let all our conversations be more and more in it. Let us all in whatsoever state or station we be in, remember ourselves to be in it. As we are gathered in our minds in it, we shall less and less desire the best of words; for *inward silence as far exceedeth the best of words as the marrow exceeds the bone.*" Certainly, as she goes on to say "the sensible knows beyond expression." But "how forcible are right words!" The spread of this Quietistic spirit amongst Friends effectually stopped the evangelistic work which marked and glorified the early years of their society. It also so dwarfed and discouraged true ministry that the marvel is that the Society survived.

Barclay's life belongs to the sad list of bright biographies as it seems to us too soon cut short by death. He died in his prime, when every year seemed to bring increased usefulness and influence for good. He was but eighteen when he was converted, but nineteen when he began to preach; his first controversial work was written when he was twenty-two, and almost the whole of his writings were produced during the next nine years, and yet they fill nine hundred folio pages!

The little band of Scottish Friends contained several remarkable men, with whom he had close and continued intercourse. For several years after his conversion, until 1673, ALEXANDER JAFFRAY (see pp. 83 & 93) survived, infirm in the body, but bright and happy in soul. His long unrest was ended; he had found amongst the Friends the close walk, the pure life, and the godly and loving brotherhood that he had long sought. The only thorns in his dying pillow were the persecuting spirit of the churches, and the non-conversion of his beloved wife. She, however, was so impressed by his death-bed experiences and testimony that she soon afterwards joined the Society. GEORGE KEITH, a graduate of Aberdeen University, was a zealous advocate of Quakerism by tongue and pen, doing and suffering with a loving zeal, on which he looked back with regretful glances after his decline and perversion. He became a Friend in 1663, and for thirty years was a pillar amongst the brotherhood. His treatises on "Immediate Revelation" and on the "Universal Light, or the Free Grace of God asserted" were highly valued by Friends. He settled in Pennsylvania; but changing his social and religious opinions, he quarreled with his brethren and with the authorities there; and after an attempt to form a new sect of "Christian Friends," he came to England and joined the established church. He was put forward as a resolute opponent of his old allies. But Gough in his History of Friends gives reasons for believing that he was conscious at the last that he had declined in grace at this time. To a Friend who visited him on his dying bed, he is reported to have said, "I wish I had died when I was a Quaker, for then I am sure it would have been well with my soul." JOHN SWINTOUNE, already mentioned, was a frequent visitor at Ury, at Monthly Meetings and other special times. Sir Walter Scott claims him as one of his ancestors. He, like Jaffray, turned from a life of political activity and honours, to a life of hearty devotion to Quakerism. He was of very good family, baron of Swintoune, and at one time one of the Lords of Sessions. He had been so mixed up with the affairs of the commonwealth, that at the Restoration he was thrown into prison, and was in great peril. But in the meantime the light of divine truth shone into his heart, and when brought to trial, he was more ready to condemn himself than his judges could be, and only anxious to tell of the goodness of God to his soul. Bishop Burnet says "He was then become a Quaker, and did with a sort of eloquence that moved the whole house, lay out his own errors, and the ill-spirit he was in, when he did the things that were charged on him, with so tender a sense, that he seemed as one indifferent what they should do with him; and without so much as moving for mercy, or even for a delay, he did so effectually prevail on them, that they recommended him to the king as a fit object for his mercy." His estates, however, seem not to have been restored to him, for in 1682 we find Robert Barclay opening his liberal purse to assist him. We have seen how useful he was to David Barclay and again to Robert Barclay at the time of their convincement; for besides his religious experience, he had, says the Biographia Brittanica, "as good an education as almost any man in Scotland, which, gained to very strong natural parts, rendered him a most accomplished person."

Amongst the pious if not prominent members of the little church at Aberdeen were Bailie Molleson and his wife. The latter died young, but her death-bed was surrounded by a halo of glory through her triumphant faith. Her daughter, Christian, had joined the Friends in her sixteenth year. She won the favourable regard and then the warm affection of the young laird of Ury, and he addressed to her the following religious love-letter.
"Dear Friend,   28th of 1st month, 1669.

Having for some time past had it several times upon my mind to have saluted thee in this manner of writing, and to enter into a literal correspondence with thee so far as thy freedom could allow, I am glad that this small occasion hath made way for the beginning of it.

The love of thy converse, the desire of thy friendship, the sympathy of thy way, and meekness of thy spirit, has often, as thou mayst have observed, occasioned me to take frequent opportunity to have the benefit of thy company; in which I can truly say I have often been refreshed, and the life in me touched with a sweet unity which flowed from the same in thee, tender flames of pure love have been kindled in my bosom towards thee, and praises have sprung up in me to the God of our salvation, for what he hath done for thee! Many things in the natural will occur to strengthen and encourage my affection toward thee, and make thee acceptable unto me; but that which is *before all and beyond all* is, that I can say in the fear of the Lord that I have received a charge from him to love thee, and for that I know his love is much towards thee; and his blessing and goodness is and shall be unto thee so long as thou abidest in a true sense of it."

After speaking of Christian contentment, " from which there is safety which cannot be hurt, and peace which cannot be broken," he warns her against the dangers to which they were both exposed from their easy circumstances, and concludes —" I am sure it will be our great gain so to be kept, that all of us may abide in the pure love of God, in the sense and drawings whereof we can only discern and know how to love one another. In the present flowings thereof I have truly solicited thee, desiring and expecting that in the same thou mayst feel and judge.   ROBERT BARCLAY."

The reader accustomed to modern Quaker phraseology, will be astonished to find it so purely spoken by so young a convert at this early date of the Society's history. But he must remember what is too often overlooked in studying the writings of the early Friends, that the Friends simply adopted in many things the religious phraseology of the times (See Barclay's Inner Life, p.

214). But he cannot fail also to be charmed with the blending of love and piety in this epistle. Within a few months of the mother's death, the young couple were married in the simple Quaker fashion. This was the first wedding of the kind in Aberdeen, and it roused in the minds of many ministers and others much unnecessary alarm and irritation. The Bishop of Aberdeen was stirred up to procure letters summoning Robert Barclay before the Privy Council for an unlawful marriage; but, says the Ury record, "the matter was so overruled of the Lord that they never had power to put their summons into execution, so as to do us any prejudice."

The conversion of the Barclays to Quakerism seems to have fanned into a flame the fires of persecution both amongst Presbyterians and Episcopalians. The Presbyterians, though suffering persecution themselves, zealously preached against the heretics, and were resolute in excommunicating all who joined them. There is a sad story of one minister who, against his own conscience, was being compelled to excommunicate his own daughter, but fell dead in the pulpit whilst pronouncing the sentence. But the clergy was especially bitter. The Bishop of Aberdeen, Patrick Scougal, and his primate, Archbishop Sharpe, were bent on extirpating the sect, and carried out the system of fine and imprisonment with the utmost vigour. Scougal (father of Henry Scougal, professor of Divinity in Aberdeen University, and whose "Life of God in the soul of man" ranks high amongst our religious classics) was too good for such dirty work. Burnet says of him, contrasting them with his scandalous brother bishops: "There was indeed one Scougal, Bishop of Aberdeen, that was a man of rare temper, great piety, and prudence, but I thought he was too much under Sharpe's conduct, and was at least too easy to him." Sharpe was just in his element in the work. A pervert from Presbyterianism for no other reason than interest, he was a suitable tool for thrusting Episcopacy on those who hated it. The wanton insults and high-handed violence which he practiced, roused the bitterest hatred on the part of the populace, and led to his murder. But from the Quakers he had no violence to fear. They would only reason, protest, and pray for him; and on a coarse spirit like his their noble Christian conduct was thrown away. At last in 1672 the declaration of indulgence cut the claws of these persecutors and gave their victims relief.

In England the Quakers had a grand service to perform for the nation, in bearing the brunt of the fierce assault made on liberty of conscience. Whilst other dissenters temporised and resorted to stratagems to conceal the fact that they still continued to meet to worship God, the Quakers openly dared the wrath of the authorities, and took gladly the penalties of their faithfulness. In Scotland this faithful service was somewhat varied. In 1662 Episcopacy was established by law, and Presbyterianism put down. But the Covenanters were not easily coerced. They took up arms in defence of their religious liberties. They met to worship God with pistols in their belts, to defend themselves from the troopers sent to break up their meetings and to arrest their preachers. The consequences were conflict and bloodshed. Loyalty to God was confounded with disloyalty to the crown. The Quakers were not slow to condemn this mode of asserting the rights of conscience. Besides complicating the issue, they deemed it inconsistent with faith in God, who was quite competent to vindicate his own cause without appeal to the sword. They set the example of passive endurance of persecution, using only spiritual and peaceful means in resisting interference with the conscience. They appealed to the consciences of their judges; they petitioned the king's council, asserting their loyalty to the throne. But whilst these assertions of loyalty and condemnations of arms won clemency from the Council, they exasperated the Presbyterians; so that in spite of the fact that they had a common foe to fight, they wasted their strength in persecuting their stoutest allies, the Quakers. In 1661 the "drunken parliament" had met in Edinbro, and vested all executive authority in the king; so that the power of the Council was unlimited. We see, then, the profligate ministers of a dissolute monarch, with Lauderdale at their head, extending protection to the Quakers whom they despised and ridiculed; and checking the rage of exasperated Covenanters, and the violence of domineering clergy.

Soon after his marriage, Robert Barclay narrowly missed a first taste of prison life. The "monthly meeting" at Aberdeen (the gathering of the local congregations for denominational business, always preceded by worship) was entered by officers sent by the magistrates to disperse the assembly. They violently dragged to the Council House all the men who were present. There the magistrates endeavoured by fair words to induce them to give up their meeting, and then let them go. If they had had more experience of Friends they would have anticipated what followed. In spite of their recent arrest, the released Friends simply returned to the meeting, and resumed their worship. Soon the officers "appeared again, and with greater fury than before dragged them back to the Council House, where the provost and council reprimanded them for contumacious resistance of civil authority, using much threatening language. But Friends were preserved in a tranquil and innocent boldness, so that 'neither the big words nor yet the barbarous deeds' of their opponents could make them flinch from an honest confession of the true reasons for their conduct." They were all sent to prison, except Patrick Livingstone, and the young laird of Ury. To the eager martyr spirit of the latter, this exemption was quite disappointing. Young as he was, and so recently married, he would gladly have shared the hardships of his brethren.

Christian Barclay became a minister of the Society of Friends, but how early we are not told. She was an admirable wife, and an exemplary mother to her seven children, all of whom not only survived their father, but by a remarkable longevity were alive fifty years after his death. She was a noted nurse, and the poor for many miles round sought her advice in sickness. No doubt she used these occasions like a true medical missionary to minister to both body and soul. She lived to be seventy-five years of age, and was greatly lamented, not only by her numerous descendants, but by the poor to whom she had been such a friend, and by the Society to which she belonged, and in whose spiritual welfare she took a deep and life-long interest.

Robert Barclay was now fairly settled with his young wife at Ury under his father's roof. His life seems to have been one of retirement and scholarly research. The fathers and theologians engaged his attention, as well as the study of the Holy Scriptures in the original tongues, so that when in 1670 he was drawn into controversy, we find him furnished with a wealth of material with which to illustrate and enforce his arguments. There has been found a MS. volume, dated 1670, consisting of controversial letters addressed by him to one of his uncles, Charles Gordon, and going over the whole ground of the Quaker controversy. This correspondence would form a valuable stepping-stone to his future work. Though his uncle died before the series of letters was complete, Barclay carried out his plan to the end, and preserved the letters on both sides as a memorial of his deceased relative.

The occasion of his first work is fully stated in its preface. In September, 1666, the Rev. Geo. Meldrum, of Aberdeen, one of the leading ministers in northern Scotland, preached a sermon specially attacking the

Quakers, towards whom he seems to have had a hatred not quite proportioned to his knowledge of them. He laid many grievous charges against them, but was suspiciously anxious that they should not get a copy of his discourse. Soon after this, proceedings were instituted to excommunicate Alexander Jaffray. But his friends raised the sound objection that no attempt had yet been made to reclaim him. So the bishop offered to confer with Jaffray in the presence of Meldrum and his colleague Menzies. But Jaffray, suspicious of one who could attack people in the dark, refused the interview unless he could have witnesses. "At length, Friends being objected to, Jaffray's brother and son who were not Friends were allowed to be present, when the Lord remarkably assisted him in declaring the truth, and defending himself and it against their unjust allegations." One result was that the Bishop directed Meldrum to give Friends a copy of the sermon preached against them, that they might reply to his statements. But instead of complying, Meldrum sent thirty Queries to be answered, and a paper entitled, "The state of the controversy between the Protestants and the Quakers." Jaffray was ill at the time, but George Keith on his behalf answered the Queries at once, and some time afterwards also replied to his paper, and to the sermon, of which they had at last obtained a copy from one of the congregation who heard it. No wonder that the future Apologist questions the honesty of the man who first condemns, and then makes enquiries, "that he might know in what things we did differ, and in what things we only seemed to differ." After giving the desired information, the Friends waited for two years for some reply, or otherwise for a retraction of the charges made. But they waited in vain. At last appeared a "Dialogue between a Quaker and a stable Christian," which Barclay ascribed to a William Mitchell, a neighbouring catechist with whom Patrick Livingstone had had some disputation. Upon him therefore Robert Barclay fell with all the energy of honest indignation, and with all the resources of a fertile and well stored mind. He entitled his book "Truth cleared of Calumnies." Though bearing the marks of a "prentice hand," many of the qualities of his later style are found in this production. William Penn says "It is written with strength and moderation." If the reader is disposed to question the moderation, he must remember the habits of the age.*

But once launched on the stormy sea of controversy, there was no more rest for him. W. Mitchell acknowledged the authorship of the "Dialogue," and returned to the attack in some "Considerations." This drew forth in rejoinder "William Mitchell unmasked," published 1672. Here we find a more mature style, a fulness of matter, and an ease and power in statement, that are only excelled in the Apology. Says the writer in the Biographia Brittanica: "In this work our author discovers an amazing variety of learning; which shows how good a use he made of his time at Paris, and how thorough a master he was of the scriptures, the fathers, and ecclesiastical history; and with how much skill and judgment he applied them." And a recent writer says "Poor William Mitchell is not only unmasked but extinguished."

Some have imagined that Robert Barclay and his friend William Penn introduced into Quakerism a new,

---

* There is in this work an interesting passage ("Truth Triumphant" pp. 29, 30), in which the view of singing held by the early Friends is set forth, which will correct some mistaken impressions. Barclay maintains "that singing is a part of God's worship, and is warrantably performed amongst the saints, is a thing denied by no Quaker so-called, and is not unusual among them, whereof I have myself been a witness, and have felt the sweetness and quickening virtue of the spirit therein, and at such occasions ministered." But they object to a mixed congregation of believers and unconverted persons singing words which in the mouths of many must be lies. (See also the Apology, Prop. ii, paragraph 26, &c.)

more reasonable, and more scholarly tone. But comparing the sixteen or eighteen years of Quakerism before these worthies accepted it, with the subsequent period when they have been supposed to affect its counsels, effectually disposes of this view. Neither in doctrine nor in practice is there any material difference. Quakerism had its scholars before them. Their pre-eminence was rather in popular gifts than in learning, and in statement and illustration of Quaker views rather than in their discovery or modification. As regards the positions of Quakerism that have given offence, Barclay and other scholarly converts accepted them in toto. They speak of the "apostacy" of the churches, and of Quakerism as the only true church. They speak boldly of the spiritual gifts of the brethren. They are severe on "hireling" priests. They argue that justification is one with sanctification. Most of the important passages referring to the authority of Holy Scripture, Barclay applies to the light within.

As to practice, nothing has more offended the proprieties of modern life than their imitations of the O. T. prophets, exhibiting themselves as signs. There is no reason to believe that any of the cultured Quakers of the day disapproved of these things; rather they rejoiced in them as part of the manifestation of the restored gifts of olden times. So far from Robert Barclay being superior to George Fox in this matter, he afforded one of the most striking instances on record. This was in 1672, and it happened thus. "On the 24th June, 1672, on awakening early in the morning, he seemed to see a great store of coined money that belonged to him lying upon his table; but several hands came and scattered it from him. Presently the scene appeared changed, and he was 'standing by a' marish' filled with a rich yellow matter, which he went about eagerly to gather in his grasp, till plunging in over the ancles, he was like to sink in the bog; then one came and rescued him. This marsh was the world, this matter was the world's goods; the whole thing was to him an intimation of love from the Lord, just as he was beginning more eagerly than before to concern himself in his outward affairs."* "The journey in sackcloth," says Mr. Gordon, "was the natural sequence of this impression." That it was "partly a penance of self-expostulation," as he further declares, we in no wise admit. We must take Barclay's own word for it that it was simply done in obedience to a clear conviction of a divine call. "The command of the Lord concerning this thing came unto me that very morning as I awoke, and the burden thereof was very great, yea, seemed almost unsupportable unto me; for such a thing until that very moment had never before entered me, not in the most remote consideration. And some whom I called to declare unto them this thing can bear witness how great was the agony of my spirit,—how I besought the Lord with tears that this cup might pass from me!—yea, how the pillars of my tabernacle were shaken, and how exceedingly my bones trembled, until I freely gave up unto the Lord's will." Truth Triumphant, p. 105.

The command was to go through three of the principal streets covered with sackcloth and ashes, calling the people to repentance. They would not listen to the voice within, nor heed the ordinary warnings of God-sent preachers. So he felt that in that terrible cross which God laid on him, He was making a more striking appeal in pity and love to their souls. He found that several of his friends approved of his obedience and were willing to go with him. So he took up his cross, and as he went on his strange errand, they felt constrained to join with him in calling the people to

---

* From the Bury Hill MSS, quoted in a remarkable article in the Theological Review of 1874, on "the Great Laird of Urie," by Alexander Gordon, M. A. The name and article suggest some family relationship with the Barclays.

repentance. No sooner was the call obeyed than his soul was filled with peace. "I have peace with my God in what I have done, and am satisfied that his requirings I have answered in this thing." His heart overflows with love as he takes up his pen to explain his procedure, and to plead with them that his appeal might not be in vain. The address is a remarkable document, full of most tender pleading and loving remonstrance. No true minister of Jesus Christ can read it without being deeply stirred, and reminded of hours when his own spirit was clothed with sackcloth and ashes for those who would not heed his warnings.

Such soul-stirrings as this, coupled with his heartfelt experience of Scripture truth, must have made Robert Barclay an able minister of Jesus Christ. He seems to have been the teacher rather than the evangelist. Probably he could no more have done George Fox's work, than George Fox could have done his. Excellently as he often writes of evangelical truth, we miss in his pages the arousing, pungent appeals of his leader. Still at this and other times he seems to have felt powerful visitations of divine grace. His brethren also now enjoyed such a gracious season that at one of the "monthly meetings," the preliminary worship was prolonged for seven hours, and the business which should have received attention afterwards had to wait until the next month. The evidences of vigorous life on all hands were most encouraging. For instance, at one of their gatherings there appeared one John Forbes, merchant of Ellon, to claim their sympathy and advice. He had adopted the Quaker views of Christian worship, and consequently had forsaken the kirk. For this he had been cited before the Presbytery of Ellon. The Friends warmly sympathised with him, and determined that Robert Barclay and certain others of their number should go to Ellon on the next Sabbath and "keep a meeting" at his house. The crowd that gathered was too great to get indoors, and doors and windows were therefore thrown open that all might hear and unite in the worship. From this beginning, the good work went on regularly every Sunday, until John Forbes had to be commissioned to look out for some more convenient place of assembly, one half of the gathering not being able to gain admittance. We have very little information of the part which Robert Barclay took in these Christian services. He kept a diary, but it seems to have been lost.* The letters of his which have been preserved are few. The most vivid and life-like impressions of the man that remain are contained in his books. These with true Quaker appreciation of the value of facts, contain many autobiographical passages, and references to his experience. To him, as to all Friends, experience was the great matter. They waited on God for clear and living views of his truth. They recognised it not by logic, but by their trained spiritual instincts. Naturally, therefore, when addressing others by tongue or pen, they preferred to be experimental rather than argumentative. But the habits of the age compelled them to be dialecticians. They could only gain a hearing by so far yielding to the popular taste. But with amusing truthfulness, William Penn says of Barclay that he adopted the scholastic style in his Apology in condescension to the weakness of literary men.

But to him this adaptation was easier than to many Friends. He was a scholar and man of letters by habit and instinct. It was a necessity of his nature that he should see clearly the whole scope and logical inferences of his principles. His intellectual fearlessness is wonderful. His learning was not idle lumber in his mind. It bore some important relation, either of agreement or of antagonism, to his views, and to the arguments of his assailants. It was either light in which he could rejoice,

---

* Is this amongst the Bury Hill MSS.? The extract quoted from the Theological Review looks like a passage from it.

or shadow which revealed some obstruction to the light, and threw out the light into bolder contrast. So learning had to him a real use and value; it was not counters but coins and the world of books was to him a very real world.

The progress of Quakerism in the neighborhood of Aberdeen, filled the hearts of many with malice that would stoop to any meanness, and carry out any iniquity. They actually demolished the walls of the Friends' burying-ground, and removed the dead bodies elsewhere; and after some subsequent interments, they kept up the practice, until stopped by the king's Council.

But it was not in Aberdeen but at Montrose that Robert Barclay first suffered imprisonment for conscience sake. It happened thus. Most of the Quakers at Kinnaber near Montrose, after being in prison for two months for the high crime of meeting together to worship God, had been released by the king's Council at the instance of John Swintoune. That gentleman and Robert Barclay sympathisingly determined to join them in their first public service, and did so. As the company was dispersing, the constables arrived, and arrested William Napier, at whose house the meeting was held, and carried him before the magistrates. Swintoune and Barclay went with him, and insisted on seeing the magistrates, and reasoning with them. On this they too were committed to prison, the ground alleged being that they had been present at the meeting. But they do not seem to have been many days in prison before the king's Council again interfered and liberated them. Whilst in prison they addressed a spirited remonstrance to the magistrates, boldly and vigorously telling them the unvarnished truth about their conduct, and appealing to them to act more righteously in future. Thus they were not behind their English brethren in the vigour with which they fought the battle of religious liberty.

In 1673 died Alexander Jaffray, whose valuable diary gives us such an interesting picture of the religious life of his time. The editor of it, John Barclay of Croydon, the laborious editor of many standard Quaker journals, found it in two parts, whilst ransacking Ury for remains of his distinguished ancestor. He published with it a sketch of the early history of Friends in Scotland, especially enriched with the substance of the minutes of the Ury meeting. Much valuable information was added in copious notes, the whole forming a precious memorial of a period of eminent spirituality and remarkable faithfulness to conscience. Jaffray's deathbed was visited by many who rejoiced in the remarkable experiences and testimony he furnished. We may be sure that the Apologist was amongst the number.

In the same year, 1673, was published Barclay's well-known Quaker Catechism. Part of its quaint title richly deserves quoting. He calls it a "Catechism and confession of faith, approved of and agreed unto by the General Assembly of the Patriarchs, Prophets and Apostles, Christ himself chief speaker in and among them." Thus he steals a march on the Assembly's Catechism on the very title-page. The object of the little book was to meet the allegation that the Quakers vilified and denied the Scriptures, by asserting their whole creed in the language of the Scriptures. The answers to the successive questions therefore are passages of Scripture without note or comment. The work is deftly done, and the Catechism has had a very large circulation.

In the next year, 1674, we find him attending the Friends' Yearly Meeting in London, then newly established, and taking part in a visit of remonstrance to the notorious Ludovico Muggleton. The only account of the interview occurs in the journal of John Gratton, the ancestor of John Bright, who was one of the party. It is interesting chiefly as indicating the hopefulness with which the early Friends tried to do good unto all men. Their patience must have been sorely tried by the ridiculous answers of the pretended prophet, whom they entrapped and exposed several times in their short interview.* Yet this is the man whom Macaulay represents as morally and intellectually the equal of George Fox.

The magistrates and clergy of Aberdeen continued specially bitter against Friends. Their preachers were imprisoned, their names published as rebels, and their goods declared forfeit to the Crown. Their meetings were disturbed with impunity by the rabble, and especially by the students of the University. This led, in February 1675, to a public dispute between some of them and Robert Barclay and George Keith. Persisting in his attempt to correct the false representations of Quakerism made by the clergy, Barclay had put forth his famous Theses Theologicæ, which played almost as important a part in the history of Quakerism as Luther's did in the Reformation. At the end of the paper he offered to defend these Theses against those who had so grossly misrepresented the teachings of Friends. The clergy, however, were not willing to meet him, but they allowed certain divinity students to accept the challenge. These young men did not regard the matter in a very serious light; it was a good joke, an opportunity to air their logic and to badger the Quakers. If other measures failed, they could rely on the mob taking their part with coarse jests, such as the cry, "Is the Spirit come yet?" Or if this treatment seemed too mild for the humour of the moment, their allies were just as ready to break the heads of the Quakers with sticks and stones. If the reader has any doubts about this description of the temper of the times, let him first read Leighton's Life, and see there the character of the ministers whom his

---

* William Penn had exposed him two years before in a pamphlet entitled, "The New Witnesses proved Old Heretics." However he still gained converts.

friends had to call in to fill up the pulpits of the ejected Presbyterians. Then after this preparation, let him read the Quaker journals of the time.

This disputation ended in uproar, the students claiming the victory of course. But the spoils were taken by the Friends in a manner little expected by the clergy. Four students, who were present at the debate, were so impressed by the arguments and christian spirit of Barclay and Keith, that they joined the Friends, and bore public testimony against the unfairness with which the debate was conducted. Here was a spiritual triumph indeed, to win trophies amidst such clamour and strife.

The dispute was not allowed to rest. The students published an account of the transaction, under the title, "Quakerism canvassed." Barclay and Keith declared the report unfair, and published theirs in self-defence. They further replied to the students in "Quakerism confirmed." Here was a field of controversy where numbers and noise were of no avail. But the termination was indeed singular. The students found that their pamphlet would not sell, and that so they were likely to be heavy losers. What was to be done? They petitioned the Commissioners for help. A little while before some of David Barclay's cattle had been seized to pay fines imposed for his attending meetings. These cattle could not be sold, so strongly did the people sympathise with the old soldier. So at last, through Archbishop Sharpe's influence, they were handed over to the students to recoup their losses!

The Theses were destined to higher honours than this farce. Dr. Nicolas Arnold, Professor of Divinity at a Dutch University, replied to them, and Barclay issued his rejoinder in Latin at Rotterdam, in 1675. Still following up the lines of thought thus opened out, the Theses were next expanded into the famous Apology, published in Latin in Amsterdam, 1676.

The years 1675 and 1676 were remarkable for a

blessed quickening of spiritual life in Aberdeen meeting. It made the Friends who were cast into prison rejoice in their bonds. It made both them and English Friends believe that the time had come when God would do great things for Scotland.*

---

* The following extracts show forth these facts and hopes with great clearness:

George Fox writes from Swarthmore, 10th of 10th month, 1675, a long letter to Robert Barclay, but evidently intended as a circular letter to Friends in Scotland. Its opening has been quoted already, pp. 84, 85. It is rich in its glowing and powerful statement of Gospel truth. After relating the vision of the condition and future blessedness of Scotland, he states how he was taken before the Council in Edinburgh and banished the nation, "but I staid three weeks after, and came to Edinburgh and had meetings all up and down." He sets forth in quaint scripture metaphors the hopes of the spiritual life which he was raised up to preach. "With the spiritual eye the virgins will see to trim their heavenly lamps, and see their heavenly olive-tree from which they have their heavenly oil, that their lamps might burn continually night and day and never go out. So that they may see the way and enter into the heavenly Bridegroom's chamber, which is above the chambers of death and imaginery." "And soe away with that chaf that would not have perfection here, for he that is perfect is risen, and that (which) is perfect is revealed." "It is the spirit of truth that leads into all truth. And they that are not led by this spirit as Christ hath sent and sends, they are led by the spirit of the false prophet, beast, whore. Though in that spirit they may profess the scriptures from Genesis to the Revelations, that spirit shall lead them into the ditch together, where they shall be consumed by God's eternal fire without the heavenly Jerusalem, as all the filth was consumed by fire without the gates of the outward heavenly Jerusalem."

"And now, Robert, concerning the things thou speaks of about thy books. I say it is well that they are sent. Keep within the rules of the spirit of Life which will lead into all truth, that all may be stirred up in your nation to walk in it, for they have been a long time asleep. For the Gospel bell does ring and sound to awaken them out of sin to righteousness. So all that have the instrument to work in God's vineyard be not idle, but be diligent that you may have your penny. For God's gospel trumpet is blown, and his alarum is sounding in his holy mountain. That makes that mind and spirit that inhabits the earth to tremble, and that they must all doe, before they inhabit and inherit eternity."

The language here may be quaint and the figures sometimes strained; but the spiritual truth is clearly seen and vigorously put, and Barclay would readily recognise its fitness to the times.

David Barclay writes to his son from Aberdeen prison on 12th of 3rd mo., 1676, in a strain of mingled trust and resignation. He writes, "we are all in health, and refreshed daily by the Lord's powerfully appearing in and amongst us, and in a wonderful and unexpected

This year (1676) seems to have been a remarkably busy one. Indeed so well was Barclay's time filled up during his short life, that one biographer most appropriately speaks of him as "posting" through the business of his life. He might almost have foreseen the early close of his career, so diligently did he redeem the time. The labours of this year included the publication of his treatise on Christian discipline entitled "The Anarchy of the Ranters," a visit to the continent, the publication of the Apology, and probably the preparation of materials for a projected history of the Christian Church. See Jaffray, p. 571.

The full title of the first-named book was, "The Anarchy of the Ranters and other libertines, the Hierarchy of the Romanists and other pretended churches, equally refused and refuted." Its object was to defend the system of discipline which the Friends had established under Fox's leadership. This system was impugned by some members as an infringement of gospel liberty. Those who were led by the Spirit, they argued, needed no rules or discipline to guide them aright, and must not have their liberty interfered with by man-made

---

way visiting us by his overcoming love to the gladdening of our hearts and making us not only to believe but to suffer for His name's sake; living praises!"

George Keith writes to Robert Barclay, also from the Aberdeen Tolbooth, "We have exceeding sweet and comfortable meetings most frequently, wherein the power of the Lord doth mightily appear in the midst of us, so that Friends generally are greatly encouraged to the astonishing and confounding of our adversaries. . . . I am busy answering H. More's papers* unto me, and have near finished my answers which I hope ere long to send unto her that is called the Lady Conway,† or else bring them myself if the persecution that is at present cease hereaway, and that I find freedom to visit Friends in England this summer. *But if the Lord open a door in this country for the receiving of the truth among people (as it is like to be, and of which we have some good expectation, the power of the Lord gloriously appearing among us, which is preparing us for some great service)* I verily believe this may be ane occasion to stay me for some time."

* See sketch of Penn, p. 54.

† From a letter of Barclay's to the Princess Elizabeth, it appears that Lady Conway in many things adopted the Quaker customs.

rules. The leader of this party was Wm. Rogers, a Bristol merchant. But his opposition was not known to Robert Barclay at the time of the publication of his treatise, though his arguments so fully anticipated their objections, that Rogers and his friends considered the book an attack on them. Feeling ran high, and Barclay was spoken of as popishly affected, if not a Papist. Yet with wonderful meekness and humility, he agreed to meet William Rogers in the presence of some trusty Friends that the offence so taken might be removed. But though the meeting resulted in Rogers acknowledging his fault, the perfect harmony of the Society was not secured by it, and he and his captious friends ultimately separated from the Society.

The treatise on Church Government is one of the best of Barclay's productions, and has been very useful, both in establishing Friends in the right development of their principles, and in enlightening other Christians as to the views they hold. One fact in connection with its publication is in perfect accord with its arguments. Three years before, there had been established in London a standing committee of the Quaker Society, called the Morning Meeting. One of its objects was to examine all writings issued by the brethren in which questions of Christian truth were discussed, so as to stamp with its approval such as were in accordance with their principles, and to disavow such as were otherwise. The necessity for such action was evident, from the fact that much annoyance and damage had been sustained by Friends, from the Society being held responsible for books written by those who were not members. Henceforth no book was to be considered an expression of the views of the Society, unless it had secured the sanction of the Committee. The "Anarchy of the Ranters" was therefore duly submitted to their scrutiny, and not only received their sanction then, but was for at least a century, published largely by the Society as an authorised statement of their views on Church discipline. Later the Yearly Meeting gave it a second title, "A Treatise on Christian Discipline." But they also struck out a passage of special interest in these times, showing how the strong reason of Barclay was logically forced along the line of Free-Churchmanship not only to Disestablishment but to Disendowment. It runs thus: "The only way then soundly to reform and remove all these abuses (i.e. those following the connection of the Church with the State) is to take away all stinted and forced maintenance and stipends, *and seeing those things were anciently given by the people, that they return again to the public treasury, and thereby the people may be greatly benefitted by them, for that they may supply for those public taxations and impositions that are put upon them, and ease themselves of them.*" *

After attending the Yearly Meeting in London, Robert Barclay went on a mission to the Continent. Of this visit, unfortunately, we have no record. Probably, one object for which he made it was to see to the publication of his Apology in Amsterdam. But one incident of the journey is full of interest. He visited Elizabeth, Princess Palatine of the Rhine, granddaughter of James I. and aunt of George I.; an accomplished lady and a most exemplary ruler. She was not only a distant relative of his (his mother and she were third cousins), but she also attracted him by her spiritual-mindedness. She had appreciated all that was best in the teachings of De Labadie, a Jesuit who turned Protestant, and by his preaching led many to seek after spiritual religion, and a simple, self-denying life.† So

---

* Barclay's "Inner Life," p. 549. This sentence is first omitted in the edition of 1765, and has been lost from the work since!

† The following note concerning De Labadie, by Whittier, the American poet, may interest the reader. "John De Labadie, a Roman Catholic priest converted to Protestantism, enthusiastic, eloquent, and evidently sincere in his special calling and election to separate the true and living members from the Church of Christ from the for-

in afterwards stating the reasons for a subsequent visit, William Penn says, "Secondly, that they (the Princess and her friends) are actually lovers and favourers of those that separate themselves from the world for the sake of righteousness. For the Princess is not only a private supporter of such, but gave protection to De Labadie himself and his company, yea when they went *under the reproachful name of Quakers*, about seven years since."*

Barclay's visit bore fruit beyond what he possibly could have foreseen. The Princess learnt heartily to esteem and love the brotherhood, welcomed the visits of its ministers, and used her influence at the English court for their relief from harassing persecution. From this time until her death she kept up a correspondence with Robert Barclay, which is included in the printed but not published Reliquæ Barclaianæ.

It would seem that this visit also afforded the opportunity for conversation with one Herr Adrian Paets,

---

malism and hypocrisy of the ruling sects. George Keith and Robert Barclay visited him at Amsterdam, and afterwards at the Communities of Herford (the Princess Elizabeth's home) and Wieward; and according to Gerard Crœse, found him so near to them on some points, that they offered to take him into the Society of Friends. This offer, if it was really made, which is certainly doubtful, was, happily for the Friends at least, declined. Invited to Herford, in Westphalia, by Elizabeth, daughter of the Elector Palatine, De Labadie and his followers preached incessantly, and succeeded in arousing a wild enthusiasm among the people, who neglected their business, and gave way to excitements and strange practices. Men and women, it was said, at the Communion drank and danced together, and private marriages or spiritual unions were formed. Labadie died in 1674, at Altona, in Denmark, maintaining his testimonies to the last. 'Nothing remains for me,' he said, 'except to go to my God. Death is merely ascending from a lower and narrower chamber to one higher and holier.'"

* He goes on to say, writing in 1677, "About a year since, Robert Barclay and Benjamin Furly took that city in the way from Frederickstadt to Amsterdam, and gave them a visit; in which they informed them somewhat of Friends' principles, and recommended the Testimony of Truth to them as both a nearer and more certain thing than the utmost of De Labadie's doctrine. They left them tender and loving." Travels in Holland, Penn's Select Works, p. 453.

Dutch Ambassador to the court of Spain, which led to the production of one of Barclay's minor works. The subject of their converse was the very soul of Quakerism, the inward and immediate revelations of the Holy Spirit. Paets stated his objections, and wished Barclay to reconsider the whole question. The Apologist did this, and was more than ever satisfied with his own position. Accordingly he wrote to Herr Paets a long letter in Latin full of subtle reasonings in his very best style, replying to the objections urged. Paets promised an answer to the letter but never sent it. However, when he met Barclay in London some years after, he acknowledged that he had been mistaken in his notions of the Quakers, for he found they could make a reasonable plea for the foundation of their religion. Barclay afterwards translated his letter into English, and published it.

This was a kind of service in which he was quite at home, and in his quiet northern home doubtless it kept him constantly employed. His English friends had not the leisure necessary to do the work in the thorough style in which he performed it. How diligently he laboured in this field, the facts already stated attest.

But the grandest fruit of his genius is undoubtedly his Apology. The address to the king is dated Nov. 25th, 1675; the Latin edition is dated Amsterdam, 1676. He was therefore only twenty-seven years of age when his masterpiece was completed; and as it was first published, so it stands to-day, unaltered. His genius matured early, though to the great perplexity of our human judgment, early maturity was followed by early death. For three or four years, his English brethren had been struggling with an unusually strong tide of misrepresentation and obloquy. He could not be a passive looker-on now that God had given him rest from persecution. He would endeavour to state the opinions of his brethren, and the rationale of them, with a fulness for which they had neither time nor opportunity. It was a brotherly and chivalrous feeling, and it had its own reward. The work was at once accepted as a standard exposition of Quakerism. It has been profusely eulogised by many who have not accepted the creed it defends. Even Voltaire has warmly praised its pure Latinity. He called it "the finest Church Latin that he knew." Sir James Mackintosh in his "Revolution in England," calls it "a masterpiece of ingenious reasoning, and a model of argumentative composition, which extorted praise from Bayle, one of the most acute and least fanatical of men." The writer in the "Theological Review," from whom we have already quoted, is enthusiastic in his admiration of it. After speaking of Rutherford's "Letters," and Scougal's "Life of God in the Soul of Man," he proceeds, "Greater, where they were greatest, than Rutherford or Scougal, was Robert Barclay; it is a country's loss that his splendid Apologia should be left in the hands of a sect. Here, indeed, is a genuine outcome of the inner depth of the nation's worship; something characteristic and her own; a gift to her religious life akin to her profoundest requirements; and if she did but know it, far worthier of the acceptance of her people than any religious aid which she has ever welcomed from the other side of the border; more satisfying to the intellect than the close scholastic conclusions of the English divines at Westminster; more full of melody to the soul than even the rude music of those ballad psalms which the Kirk had not been too proud to adapt from the version of the Cornish statesman. One great original theologian, and only one, has Scotland produced; he it is the history of whose life and mind we shall endeavour to approach in the present Article." Theol. Review, 1874, p. 528.

We must not leave the Apology without referring to its manly and honest preface. It has been praised as heartily as the book itself. In an age of fulsome flattery, it is unique in its appeal to the better nature of King Charles, whom the writer begs not to despise the singular mercies which God had shown him. On Barclay's return to London from Holland, he probably presented a copy to the king; and it is to the credit of that monarch that, far from taking offence at the plain speaking of his Quaker kinsman, we find him ever after showing him special favour. Penn and Barclay seem alike to have possessed the power of drawing out the best side of the characters of Charles II. and his brother James II This fact must be borne in mind in considering the charges laid against the former because of intimate relations with the Court.

From the Continent, Barclay returned to London, where he heard that his father and other of his Aberdeen friends had been thrown into prison for "holding conventicles." He immediately began to devise measures for their release. He had a letter from the Princess Elizabeth to her brother Prince Rupert. He presented this, met of course with a civil reception, and took the opportunity to obtain the Prince's concurrence with a petition which he was presenting to the king. He also wrote to the Princess to support his application, and then presented his petition. His plea is that a difference should be made between the peaceable and loyal Quakers, and those against whom the laws were directed. Unfortunately Prince Rupert was indisposed, and unable to keep his promise. So as the petition was vigorously opposed, his memorial was passed on to the Scotch Privy Council, with such a cool endorsement that it took no effect.

It was on this errand that he first sought the Duke of York, afterwards James II. He himself has told the story in his "Vindication." "Being at London and employed by my friends to obtain a liberty for them out of their imprisonment at Aberdeen for the single exercise of their conscience, and not being able to gain any ground upon the Duke of Lauderdale, in whose hands was the sole management of Scots affairs at that time, I was advised by a Friend to try the Duke of York, who was said to be the only man whom Lauderdale would bear to meddle in his province, or who was like to do it with success. And having found means of access to him, I found him inclined to interpose in it, he having then and always since to me professed himself to be for liberty of conscience. And though not for several years, yet at last his interposing proved very helpful in that matter."

The reply of the Princess Palatine to Robert Barclay's request, is interesting as a specimen of the religious correspondence of these illustrious friends. She says, "Your memory is dear to me, so are your lines and exhortations very necessary. I confess also myself spiritually very poor and naked; all my happiness is, I do know I am so, and whatever I have studied or learnt heretofore is but dirt in comparison with the true knowledge of Christ. I confess my infidelity to this Life heretofore, by suffering myself to be conducted by false, politic lights. Now that I have sometimes a small glimpse of the true Light, I do not attend it as I should, being drawn away by the works of my calling, which must be done; and as your swift English hounds I often overrun my scent, being called back when it is too late."

In his reply, Barclay tells of the non-success of his efforts to obtain the release of his friends, and yet adds with calm heroism, " I this day take my journey towards them, not doubting but I shall also share their joys." Nor was he mistaken. Soon after reaching Aberdeen, he was arrested and placed in the Tolbooth. This gaol was divided into two parts, the lower, which was vile, the upper, which was worse. Robert Barclay was allowed a place in the lower prison, but those who were arrested with him were thrust into the upper prison. Here shortly afterwards they were joined by David Barclay, who had been released only to fall again into the clutches of the enemy.

Th enews of Robert Barclay's commitment to prison reached his royal friend Elizabeth the next month (Dec. 1676). She at once wrote to console him. "I am sure that the captivers are more captive than you are, being in the company of him that admits no bonds, and is able to break all bonds." She also wrote at once to her brother Prince Rupert to use his influence with the king on his behalf.

Her letter put the case plainly and well. "I wrote you some months ago by Robert Barclay who passed this way, and hearing I was your sister, desired to speak with me. I knew him to be a Quaker by his hat, and took occasion to inform myself of all their opinions; and finding they were accustomed to submit to magistrates in real things, omitting the ceremonial, I wished in my heart the King might have many such subjects. And since I have heard that notwithstanding his Majesty's most gracious letters in his behalf to the Council of Scotland, he has been clapped up in prison with the rest of his friends, and they threaten to hang them, at least those they call preachers among them, unless they subscribe their own banishment; and this upon a law made against other sects that appeared armed for the maintenance of their heresy; which goes directly against the principles of those which are ready to suffer all that can be inflicted, and still love and pray for their enemies. Therefore, dear brother, if you can do anything to prevent their destruction, I doubt not but you will do an action acceptable to God Almighty, and conducive to the service of your royal master. For the Presbyterians are their violent enemies, to whom they are an eyesore, as being witnesses against all their violent ways. I care not though his Majesty see my letter. It is written out of no less an humble affection for him, than most sensible compassion for the innocent sufferers."

Besides writing this letter she agreed to use her influence with Lady Lauderdale, and to get her brother to do his best with the Earl, but she explains she has little expectation of success as they are no friends of theirs.

This letter and other influences led to a royal recommendation to the King's Council in Edinbro', but some interval elapsed before it bore fruit. Meanwhile, the father and son had been removed to a gaol outside the town, called the Chapel. Their treatment here was malicious enough, but mild in comparison with what many of their brethren suffered; and though they protested, as became Britons and Quakers, no doubt they thanked God for the comparative ease of their lot. Whilst in prison they received many letters of sympathy from their friends. Amongst these is a little known letter from William Penn, hoping that they "may grow spiritual soldiers, expert and fitted by these exercises for such spiritual conflicts as the Lord hath for you to go through;" and that they may grow "as trees in winter, downwards, that your root may spread; so shall you stand in all storms and tempests."

One of the excuses for ill-using the Friends was that they were Popishly affected. This must have galled Robert Barclay's sensitive nature exceedingly. His growing friendship with the King and the suspected Duke of York gave colour to the charge, and his training in a Catholic college, his former profession of the Catholic faith, and his near kinship to many Catholics, were taunts ready to the hand of disputants like the Aberdeen students or the scurrilous John Brown.

From the "Chapel," Barclay wrote a strong appeal to Archbishop Sharpe to abandon his unchristian persecutions. Does the reader think this is like asking Shylock to renounce his pound of flesh? He must remember that the Quakers were accustomed to accomplish such impossibilities; and where their hardy faith could not succeed in such feats, it could persevere in attempting them. Their love was as invincible as their patience. They sincerely pitied their persecutors, and felt that they were harming themselves more than they hurt the Friends. So for their soul's sake they pleaded with them, using every argument which they thought they could ask God to bless. Whilst in Aberdeen prison, Barclay also wrote his treatise on "Universal Love," an earnest plea for religious toleration.

The prisoners gained their liberty by an amusing disagreement between the Aberdeen Magistrates and the Sheriff, which led to a lawsuit. Meanwhile, Robert Barclay and others who had been liberated on parole, went before a notary and claimed their full liberty.

We now find Robert Barclay attending the Yearly Meeting in London, and then going on to the Continent in company with George Fox and William Penn. Their object was two-fold, aggression and organisation. The Mennonite churches of the Netherlands and Germany were the special attraction. William Caton, at one time tutor at Swarthmoor Hall, had settled in Holland, and had met with a cordial welcome amongst these churches. William Ames and other Friends also visited them, and by degrees the Quakers had become very strong in Holland. William Penn had visited them before. We may here remark that the Friends have ever kept up a kindly and brotherly intercourse with the Mennonites whether in Germany, Russia, or the United States, visiting them for fraternal encouragement, and helping them in times of famine and persecution.

Considering that both of Barclay's companions kept diaries which have since been published, it is remarkable how little we learn of him from their records. Penn's narrative is a rich spiritual treat, but would have been richer had it been his purpose to tell of the private as well as of the public transactions of the "three great apostles of the sect," as Hepworth Dixon calls them.

What glorious times of spiritual communion they must have had. With strongly marked individuality, there was yet a genuine bond of union and true sympathy between them. Fox, the senior by twenty years, was strongest in acquaintance with the facts about the state of the Society. His faulty English might at times jar on the ears of his scholarly brethren, but that was less offensive to them than the impure spiritual dialects of many professed Christians. His strong and many-sided nature enabled him to meet Penn in his large philanthropic schemes, and to sympathise with Barclay in his scholarly labours. If already his frame was feeling the effects of much suffering whilst his brethren were in their prime, his soul knew no decay. Penn might be the strongest of the three on the point of leavening earthly institutions with heavenly aims. Barclay's surpassing intellectual gifts might forbid any man to despise his youth. But in deep spiritual life they were equals. What mighty wrestlings must have been theirs as they talked of the spiritual needs of the world! How they must have exulted in the progress of spiritual truth! Their own Society at the time probably numbered at least 50,000 members. There were many not of their community with whom they held sweet intercourse through a common enjoyment of spiritual religion. Their faith was unfaltering that a new era had dawned upon the Christian church, which was about to renew its youth, and repeat the glorious triumphs of its early days.

After successfully organising in Holland the same system of church government which had been set up in England, they visited Herford, the court of the Princess Elizabeth. Barclay had written to her from Aberdeen prison, strongly urging her, since she felt the power and blessing of silent waiting on God, to trust that, and especially to dismiss her "hireling" chaplain with his "unallowable services." In reply she had pleaded that the way was not yet plain to her; she must wait for light. If only her faith were strengthened what might she not do? But the result did not answer Barclay's expectation. They had, indeed, times of great spiritual refreshment, and the right hand of the Lord was revealed, but the Princess was not won to silent worship, nor to renounce the ordinary modes of worship. However Barclay urges and pleads with her, her reply still is "I must go by my light." "I cannot submit to the opinions or practice of others, though they have more light than myself."*

At Herford, Barclay left his friends and returned to Amsterdam. In September we find him in London, using his influence with the Duke of York to procure liberty for Friends in Scotland. He only succeeded, however, so far as his father and himself were concerned. When he wrote the result to his friend the Princess, and after shewing the dangers that awaited him, told her he was returning to Scotland, she was astonished, and warmly remonstrated with him for taking such a course. Robert Barclay had expressed sorrow at her non-success. She tells him that it is no cross to her that Lady Lauderdale returns no other answer to her request than a mere court compliment, and proceeds:—" But it is a cross to me that you will not make use of the liberty which God miraculously gave you, but will return into Scotland to be clapt up again into prison, for which we have neither precept nor example." But to stop in the path of duty because there were dangers ahead, would have been a failure of obedience which would have plunged Barclay's soul into darkness and distress. He must go forward and leave the consequences to God.

The persecution of the Aberdeen Friends continued unabated until 1679. In the spring of that year Arch-

---

* Not that Barclay aimed at proselytising, but he wished her to take the course which seemed to him the necessary outcome of her views. "I pretend to be no sect master," he writes, "and disgust all such."

bishop Sharpe, the chief instigator of it, was assassinated, and Lauderdale removed from office; and immediately came a lull in the storm. In November, Robert Barclay and some others were indeed thrown into prison, but they were released in a few hours. The favour of the Council towards Friends in general, and especially the interest at court of Robert Barclay, were too strong for the persecutors, and they capitulated. Locally the hard fought fight was won.

The royal favour was still more distinctly shown to Robert Barclay when, in the same year, the Ury estate was, by royal charter dated 14th August, erected into a barony, with civil and criminal jurisdiction to himself and his heirs forever. This was about the time when James was made Lord High Commissioner, and being jealous of the influence of Monmouth, was nursing his Scotch popularity. In the act of parliament (1685) confirming the charter, it is said to be granted "for the many services done by Colonel David Barclay and his son the said Robert Barclay to the king and his most royal progenitors in times past." It was swept away, with all kindred privileges, when George II. remodelled the government of Scotland. But the Court Book is still in existence to bear testimony to his conscientious administration of justice.

In this year he also paid another visit to Holland, but was unable to visit his royal correspondent the Princess Elizabeth at Herford. However he wrote her what proved to be a final letter, dated Rotterdam, 6th of the 5th month, 1679. In this characteristically sensitive but affectionately faithful epistle, he says, "Thou may think strange that after so long a silence I should now apply myself to answer thy last (which came to my hands at a time when I was under great bodily weakness) for which I will not trouble thee with any further Apologie than to assure thee that no want of respect or regard to thee, but ane unwillingness to work in mine own will, and a fear in so doing rather to hurt than help thee, hath hindered me until now. Had I given way to my own inclinations, and to the course of that love, which, without flattery I can say I have for thee, so as to have exprest but the hundred part of that concern which frequently possessed me on thy account, I had overcharged thee with my letters. But knowing it is not the will of man that bringeth about the work of God, I choosed rather to be silent than forward. But being through a singular occasion come to this country, and not having access to make thee a visit, I found a true liberty from the Lord in my spirit thus to salute thee." From what follows it seems that either the Princess misunderstood his anxious solicitude for her, or he thought she did. His apology for his urgency is touching. He concludes; "For herein I have peace before God, that I never sought to gather thee nor others to myself, but to the Lord. I pretend to be no sect master, and disgust all such. My labour is only as an ambassadour to instruct all to be reconciled to God, and desire no more than to be manifest in the consciences of those to whom I come that I am such, by the answer of that of God there, to which therefore in my conscience I recommend my testimony." In not seeing the Princess on this visit he missed his last opportunity, for she died the following year. Penn has paid a tribute to her memory in "No Cross, No Crown," in which he says, "I must needs say her mind had a noble prospect; her eye was to a better and more lasting inheritance than can be found below, which made her often despise the greatness of courts, and learning of the schools, of which she was an extraordinary judge."

To this year also belong two of his writings—a "duply" to a scurrilous reply to his Apology, entitled "Quakerism the pathway to Paganism," by John Brown, and a translation of his Latin letter to the Ambassadors assembled at Nimeguen, urging the claims of peace.

During the remaining years of his life, Robert Barclay published little. Probably he was too busy to write much. Of his employments unfortunately we know little. His writings, his learning, his great ability, his rank, his aristocratic friends and connections, and his influence at court, made him a man of mark. In his own society, he was a recognised leader. His ministry evidently was of a high order. Possibly not so popular as that of Fox or Penn, it must have been solid, earnest, and impressive. He is known to us almost solely as an author, but his own generation knew him as a capable man of affairs. He was not a popular leader like Fox, or a man consumed by large humanitarian schemes like Penn. But he had a broad and liberal mind, sound judgment, and an insinuating address. The dedication of the Apology shows with what skill he could walk on delicate ground.

About this time, the divisions which troubled Friends in England found their way to Aberdeen. Rogers and Bugg sent their slanderous letters everywhere, and as Barclay was mistakenly supposed to have written the "Anarchy of Ranters" against the former, it was not likely that the peace of Aberdeen would be undisturbed. Several members had to be expelled and then harmony was restored. It is to this that the following extract from a letter of George Fox refers.

"London, 31st of 4th mo. (June), 1680.
"Dear Robert Barclay,

With my love to thee and thy Father and all the rest of the faithful friends in the holy peaceable truth, that is over all and changes not. I am sorry to hear that there should be any difference or distance amongst any Friends in your parts, and that they should not keep in the power of the Lord to the spreading of the truth abroad, and such great want and need as there is in your country. For all should be in the Gospel of peace, in the power of God in which enmity cannot come, and in the peaceable wisdom which is easy to be entreated. And therefore you that are ministers in that nation should meet together sometimes, and keep in unity, and that you might treat of things that tend for peace, as the Apostles and Elders did in their day, to the establishing, settling, and preserving of the churches in Christ Jesus."

It may surprise some who have mistaken ideas of Fox's methods to find him saying: "I shall write a few words to John Blaikling, for him and Thomas Langhorn to come into your country, for they are honest men and may be very serviceable." From the next sentence, it appears that Barclay had not been at the recent Yearly Meeting which had threatened to be a stormy one, but had passed off peaceably. "As for the Yearly Meeting, the Lord did manifest his wonderful power and presence in all the meetings, and it was mighty large from all parts, and the love of God was raised in Friends beyond words. I have not seen the like. And though many of the dirty spirits was there that are rebellious, yet the Lord's power and truth was over them, and Friends parted in the power and love of God, and all was quiet."

In 1679–1682 the Duke of York was in Scotland, first as Lord High Commissioner, afterwards on a visit. Considering the cruel and mischievous policy which he pursued there, it seems incredible to us that Barclay should have been able to like him. Yet he seems often to have been at his court, and to have had the favourable impressions which he had already received of the duke deepened and confirmed. Hume says indeed that, "the duke had behaved with great civility towards the gentry and nobility [of Scotland] and by his courtly demeanour had much won upon their affections." So that Barclay was not alone. At one time he verified before the duke a claim of his father's for money laid out in the service of Charles I.; the debt was acknowledged, but only a small part, less than £300, was ever paid. Again he visits him in Edinbro' at the earnest desire of William Penn about the New Jersey affairs.* At other times he fully used his great influence with James on behalf of his friends. Even when in 1680 the Duke was called to Windsor, Barclay's wishes were not forgotten as appears by the following note.

Windsor, June 27th, 1680.

I send you here enclosed a letter to the Lord Advocate as you desired. I choose to write to him because I had spoken to him of it when I was in Scotland. You see I do my part, and I make no doubt but that he will do his, and then you will have no further trouble in that affair.   JAMES.

Whilst in London in 1682, Robert Barclay was appointed governor of East Jersey (the Eastern part of New Jersey) which had been purchased by William Penn, the Earl of Perth, and other of his friends. He was made one of the proprietors, and " to induce him to

---

* The whole letter which tells us this is worth quoting. Letters of the Early Friends, pp. 257, 8.

Edr. [Edinburgh], the 10th mo. [Dec.] 1679.

DEAR G. F.,

To whom is my dear and unfeigned love in the unchangeable Truth, of whom to hear is always refreshful to me. I know it will be acceptable to thee to understand that at last the tedious persecution at Aberdeen seems to have come to an end, for Friends have had their meetings peaceable near these two months, and dear P. L. (Patrick Livingstone) after having had several peaceable meetings, is now come away a noble conqueror from that place, and is gone to visit Friends in the west country, and then intends homeward by way of Newcastle. I doubt not, but that God will abundantly reward his courage and his patience; for his stay hath been of great service to Truth and Friends in these parts.

I came here at the earnest desire of W. P. (William Penn) and other Friends to speak to the Duke of York concerning the New Jersey business; but fear there will be little effectual got done in it. I doubt it has been spoiled in the managing at first. * * * I should be very glad, if thy freedom could allow of it, to see thee in this country in the spring. I know it would be of great service, for there are several things that would need it. Several things go cross, and are so now in divers places; and I know no man's presence could so easily remedy it as thine." He signs himself, " thy real friend, R. BARCLAY."

accept thereof [of the Governorship] they gifted him a propriety with 5000 acres *more* for him to bestow as he should think fit." "Charles II. confirmed the grant of the Government, and the royal commission states that 'such are his known fidelity and capacity, that he has the Government during life; but no other governor after him shall have it longer than three years.'" He appointed as his deputy Gawen Laurie, a London Friend and merchant, already attached to the province as one of the proprietors of West Jersey. His brothers John and David intended to settle there, but David died on the voyage. He was a youth of great piety and promise, greatly beloved, especially by his father. John settled at Perth-Amboy, the capital of the province, where he died in 1731. The only mention of him which I can find is in Smith's History of New Jersey, where it is said, "He bore the character of a good neighbour, and was very serviceable to the public in several capacities, but more particularly in Amboy, where he lived and died."*

In Robert Barclay, William Penn would have not only a practical adviser, but one able to understand and sympathise with his lofty aims. He who suggested two hundred years ago a just method of disendowment, and who so effectively advocated the cause of peace, would have large-hearted sympathy and suggestions for the founder of the Western Utopia. It is unfortunate that we have no information of his plans and efforts for the two colonies. Once only the curtain is lifted. In 1685 we find him "attentive to the welfare of East Jersey by shipping provisions and engaging indented servants in Aberdeen." †

---

* Both brothers were members of the Society of Friends, and the younger was already a minister at the time of his death.

† Education was early attended to by Friends. "In 1681 in Aberdeen Monthly Meeting, two schools were established, one for boys and one for girls. The latter was held in the meeting-house. The schoolmistress was besought by the church 'to seek to accomplish herself

There is a well-known and authentic story of Barclay's adventure with a robber, which is often quoted by Friends in support of their belief in non-resistance to evil. He had been to London, and had left one of his sons at Theobalds, where his old friend George Keith had set up a school. One morning his wife noticed that he looked thoughtful, and asked the reason. He replied that he believed some uncommon trial would that day befal the company. They set out on their journey, and met with the not uncommon incident in those days near London—an attack from highwaymen. One of these presented his pistol at Robert Barclay, who with calm self-possession took him by the arm, and asked him how he came to be so rude. The robber dropped his pistol, and became quiet as a lamb. Mrs. Barclay's brother was not so fortunate, he was robbed; and one of the four members of the party, a Dutchman named Sonmans, accidentally received a wound in his thigh from which he died. Surely the father never showed more coolness under fire than did the son when suddenly confronted by such danger.*

---

in reading, writing, and arithmetic,' and also to get 'a good stocking-weaver.' The church also, 'had a true sense that there is cause for encouraging her.' Some of the parents thought otherwise and withdrew their children, and it was directed, that they be weightily dealt with to return them again. The boys school had a schoolmaster who was allowed 100 pound rent. It was to impart 'the Latin tongue and other commendable learning.' The 'priests' manifested 'great trouble' at the setting up of this school, because 'several considerable people of the world have sent their children thereto, highly commending their profiting therein beyond their own schools. And some fruits also as to conviction and conversion among the young ones hath been of great encouragement to us.'' (Robert Barclay's "Inner Life, &c.," p. 482, note.)

That Robert Barclay took great interest in this effort may be taken for granted. There is extant a copy of a letter of his widow's (dated 15th of 6th mo., 1693) full of earnest desires for the scholars and recommendations to the teachers.

* The incident is thus told more fully and picturesquely by Wilson Armistead. "Calm and self-possessed, he looked the robber in the face, with a firm but meek benignity, assured him he was his and every man's friend, that he was willing and ready to relieve his wants;

Barclay like William Penn was charged with doubtful relations with James II. They both believed him sincere in his professed regard for religious liberty; they both felt for him a real, though it seems to us an unmerited regard. He showed them both special kindness, and listened to their pleas for their brethren and for others. George Fox writes to Barclay in 1686:—"Friends were very sensible of the great service thou hadst concerning the truth with the king and all the court; and that thou hadst their ear more than any Friend when here." But it must not be supposed that they were therefore indifferent to the constitutional principles at stake. (See sketch of Penn.) There is a curious disproof of this in a hint conveyed in the Friends' address to the king on his Declaration of Indulgence, drawn up by the Yearly Meeting of 1687, when it is almost certain that Barclay was present and must have concurred. "We hope," they say, "the good effects thereof may produce such a concurrence from the parliament as will secure it to our posterity." This influence at court caused Robert Barclay often to be wanted in London, and he seems to have been a constant attender of the Yearly Meetings up to 1688.

In 1685 we are told that Barclay was again in London at the Yearly Meeting, and employed himself in many acts of kindness. Charles II. had died on the 6th of February, and James at once ascended to the throne. If Barclay had been anxious for the royal favour, as some asserted, he would at once have gone to

---

that he was free from the fear of death through a divine hope of immortality, and therefore was not to be intimidated by a deadly weapon, and then appealed to him whether he could find in his heart to shed the blood of one who had no other feeling or purpose but to do him good. The robber was confounded; his eye melted; his brawny arm trembled; his pistol dropped out of his hand on to the ground, and he fled from the presence of the non-resistant hero whom he could no longer confront." Mr. Armistead's memoir was published long after the publication of the contemporary letters which give the simpler narrative; the reader must take his choice.

court to salute the rising sun. Instead, we find him going simply to the May gatherings of his brethren, and only at a later date seeking the royal presence on behalf of others.

In 1686 he repeated his visit on the same errand and took part with George Whitehead in an appeal to the king, which resulted in the liberation of 1200 Friends. Whitehead says he took Barclay with him, "the king having a particular respect for him from the knowledge he had of him in Scotland;" but Whitehead seems to have been the chief speaker. In the end the king granted a commission to the attorney-general, Sir R. Sawyer, to issue warrants to release all whom he could legally discharge as the king's prisoners, which through George Whitehead's energy was thoroughly carried out.

Soon after Barclay's return, his aged father sickened, and died on the 12th of October. His son published a very full account of his last days, which seem to have been full of heavenly calm and restful faith. The old soldier, after a youth of adventures and a manhood of perils and persecutions, "fell asleep," says his son, "like a lamb." The feelings that first won him to Quakerism were strong to the last. To the doctor who attended him he said, "It is the *life* of righteousness that we bear witness to, and not an empty profession." To the Friends who gathered round his dying-bed, he said, "How precious is the love of God among his children, and their love to one another! My love is with you— I leave it among you." As the end drew near, he exclaimed, "Now the time comes! Praises, praises to the Lord! Let now thy servant depart in peace." And so he crossed the river.

Again in 1687 Robert Barclay visited London, travelling with Viscount and Lady Arbuthnot, the latter as a daughter of the Earl of Sunderland being a distant cousin of his own. The Scotch Quakers had previously met in Aberdeen, and had drawn up in their

General Meeting an address of acknowledgment to the king on his recent Declaration of Indulgence; this Robert Barclay presented. A similar one, prepared by this London Yearly Meeting of 1687 and presented to the king by William Penn, has been already mentioned. On this occasion, Barclay visited the seven bishops who were in the Tower for refusing to circulate this very Declaration. They had declared that the Quakers had belied them by reporting that they had been the death of some of them. Probably Barclay felt not only that the charge, which certainly had been made, must be sustained for the credit of his brethren, but what was more important, that the bishops were now in a position better to understand the Quaker pleas for liberty of conscience. So he produced to them unquestionable proof that some Friends had been kept in gaol until they died, even after trustworthy physicians had warned their persecutors that death must be the result of their longer detention. However, he assured them that they would not publish the damaging facts, lest it should furnish a handle to their enemies.

His last visit to London was early in 1688, and he remained all the summer. On the journey he had the company of his brother-in-law, Sir Ewen Cameron, of Lochiel. He took with him his eldest son Robert, then a boy of sixteen, remarkable alike for his piety and for his precocious Scotch prudence, and introduced him to the court at Windsor. There he remained for some time, "being much caressed, it is said, on account of his father's interest, which occasioned numerous dependents; and he appears to have conducted himself so as to incur no reproach even with Quakers." A sermon which Robert Barclay preached at this time in Gracechurch St. Meeting, was reported and has been published. One great object of this journey was to see justice done to his brother-in-law, who had a difference with the powerful Duke of Gordon. Barclay set himself in good earnest to get the matter righted. First he wrote to several English noblemen with whom he was intimate, but they were shy of the difficult task, though they all professed their willingness to help him in anything else. Then he appealed to the king, and "succeeded in obtaining from him a full hearing upon the whole matter, in the presence of the Marquis of Powis and the Earls of Murray and Melfort, who were requested to become referees. Persevering through all obstructions raised by the opposite party, Barclay was able at length to obtain a final settlement, much to the advantage of Cameron of Lochiel." Thus again James appears under Barclay's influence as the good genius of the oppressed.

On one of his visits to the court, he found the king full of the thought of the coming of the Prince of Orange. They had a serious conversation about the state of affairs, and Barclay, like Penn, sincerely sympathised with the royal culprit in his troubles. "Being with him near a window, the king looked out and observed that 'the wind was then fair for the Prince of Orange to come over.' Robert Barclay replied, 'it was hard that no expedient could be found to satisfy the people.' The king declared he would do anything becoming a gentleman, except parting with liberty of conscience, which he never would whilst he lived."

After the Revolution, the calumnies by which he was assailed led to his drawing up a "Vindication," which is the last known production of his pen. For himself he would have been content to bear these calumnies in silence. Two reasons overruled this choice. Some men of judgment who found how completely he could refute them, wished his answers to be well known. On the other hand, the loss of his reputation caused damage to the Society to which he belonged, and of whose interests he was so jealous. Yet his own contempt for the charges laid against him, and for the popular opinion of him, is evident in almost every paragraph. There is more than courageous outspokenness; there is the indifference of one who feels, "With me it is a small thing that I should be judged of you. He that judgeth me is the Lord."

He sums up the charges against him thus:—"That I am a papist and some will needs have me a Jesuite; that the access and interest I have been thought to have had with the king is thereto ascribed; that I have been a great caballer and councealor of those things that have been done for the advancement of the Romish interest and agrieving of the people: and thence have been a joint contriver with the Jesuit Peters and others; and that for this I have received advantages and money from the king, and so consequently am chargeable with the odium and censure that such doings merit." To this he replies, that he has been married eighteen years and has several children, which proves him no Jesuit; that for twenty-two years he has been no Papist, "without being under the least temptation to return to it again;" that he has always avowed his opposition to those principles "in the opinion of some more forwardly than prudently," when the catholic party was strong, "judging it," he adds sarcastically, "a fitter season then than now to show zeal for the Protestant religion." The only money ever paid to him from the treasury is acknowledged in the published accounts, and so on. But what is most daring is his charity towards the fallen monarch and his Catholic friends in the hour of their unpopularity. "For I must confess that the fatal stroaks the interest of the Church of Rome seems to have gotten in these nations does not a whitt increase my aversion to their religion, for that I judge truth and error is not rightly measured by such events; and as to the persons of Roman Catholics, as it never agreed with the notions I have of the Christian religion to hate these persons, so their present misfortunes are so far from embittering my spirit towards them that it rather increases tenderness and regard to them, while I consider the ingenerous spirit of those who cannot take a more effectual way to lessen the reputation of the Protestant religion."

"I come now to the great charge of my access to and interest with the king. And if I should ask whether that were a crime? I find few reasonable men, if any, would say so. But I am neither afraid nor ashamed to give a candid account of that matter." He then gives the occasion of their meeting in 1676, as narrated elsewhere, and proceeds:—" To do him right, I never found reason to doubt his sincerity in the matter of liberty of conscience. . . . After his happening to be in Scotland, giving me an opportunity of more frequent access, and that begetting an opinion of interest, I acknowledge freely that I was ready to use it to the advantage of my friends and acquaintances, what I esteemed just and reasonable for me to meddle in." Again he says, "In short I must own nor will I decline to avow that I love King James, that I wish him well, that I have been and am sensibly touched with a feeling of his misfortunes, and that I cannot excuse myself from the duty of praying for him that God may bless him, and sanctify His afflictions to him. And if so be His will to take from him an earthly crown, He may prepare his heart and direct his steps so that he may obtain through mercy an heavenly one, which all good Christians judge the most preferable."

The last two years of Robert Barclay's life seem to have been spent in social enjoyment and quiet usefulness at home. "There," we are told, "his mild and amiable virtues found their happiest sphere of exercise, and he enjoyed the esteem of his neighbours." But such serene happiness was not to last. In 1690, he travelled in the ministry in the north of Scotland, accompanied by another Quaker preacher named James Dickinson. Soon after his return home, he was seized with a violent fever, under which he soon sunk, and died on the 3rd of October, 1690. He was laid beside his father in the vault in the burial place in the beautiful grounds of Ury which his father had prepared. (Thither his descendants and namesakes were gathered one by one for 160 years, until in 1854, the last laird, Capt. Barclay-Allardice, after mortgaging his estates to their full value, and bringing sadness to the hearts of all who loved the name he bore, was brought there to his last rest.) There was great lamentation, especially in his own society, when the news got abroad. Fox, Penn, and others bore no grudging testimony to his gifts and services. The latter edited his works, with an ample preface, in which the subjects and merits of the different treatises are spoken of with judgment, yet with all the warmth of a personal friend.

Barclay's Apology has been spoken of as a system of Divinity. It is nothing of the kind, but simply an exhaustive treatise on the points in which Quakerism differs from the current evangelical Christianity of his day. The point is of importance, because otherwise the reader may be led astray both by the omissions from the work, and by the proportions allotted to different subjects. He must look elsewhere, for instance, for proofs that the early Friends were substantially orthodox in their views of the Trinity.

Much has been said about the Apology being framed on a plan similar to the Assembly's Catechism, and being indeed a reply to it. But that Catechism itself is on the plan of Calvin's Institutes, the trusted guide of Scotch orthodoxy. It would be an interesting point to trace the relation between the Institutes and the Apology. As to the Calvinistic controversy, a recent writer says, "No man ever gave Calvinism such mighty shakes as Barclay did. And he shook it from within. He understood it. As the religion of his country he had entered into it and made himself master of it. His controversy with Calvin was on fundamental principles." (Theological Review, 1874, p. 553). These assertions must be modified by remembering that, as we have seen, almost from childhood Barclay disliked Calvinism, so that whilst he might effectually combat some of its positions, he was little likely to do justice to its strong points, and can hardly be said to have shaken it from within. The Arminianism of the Catholic Church would strengthen his instinctive dislike, so that though he found the Quakers Arminians, he in nowise owed his convictions on this point to them.

The style of the Apology is beautifully clear. The best proof of its simplicity is to be found in the fact that many of the artisan class have so followed its reasonings as to be led to accept Quakerism by this book alone. Probably it has brought more converts to Quakerism than any other book that ever was written. It is grand in its efficient handling of great questions without any appearance of labour or effort. There is a cumulative power in many of the paragraphs that is very effective; epithet piled on epithet, clause following up clause like the waves of the incoming tide, until mind and heart are alike borne along by its rush. The thought is made to stand out not only boldly and clearly, but clothed with that subtle power which is only wielded by the transparently honest and the intensely earnest. At times the writer condescends to brusque vehemence or touching appeal to his own experience.

Whatever claim for originality of thought is advanced on behalf of Robert Barclay, must principally be based on his arguments in defence of Quakerism, and on his systematising of Quaker thought.* His namesake and

---

* In the "Yorkshireman," a religious paper conducted by the eminent meteorologist, Luke Howard, F.R.S., before he left the Society of Friends, in consequence of their action in the "Beacon" controversy—there is (vol. III. pp. 8–14) an interesting enquiry as to Barclay's indebtedness to George Keith for his views as to the "hypothesis or system relating to the 'Seed or Birth of God in the soul,' which

descendant, the late Robert Barclay of Reigate, bestowed great pains and labour on investigations to find out how far the ideas of the Early Friends were known to the world before George Fox preached them. He has shewn in his "Inner Life of the Religious Societies of the Commonwealth" that to a large extent the religious phrases and tenets of the Friends, were those used and held by Caspar Schwenkfeld, and his followers amongst the Mennonite churches of Holland and Germany. Churches of their faith and order were established in York and Lincoln when George Fox began to preach, through which he may have received their views.*

At least Mr. Barclay has proved that Fox was acquainted with these views, though possibly he may not

---

makes it a distinct being or substance as the Vehiculum Dei, &c.'" The writer terms Barclay's view a Platonising doctrine. Certainly Keith felt very kindly towards Dr. Henry More, the great Platonist, and urged Friends to shew him loving sympathy "notwithstanding of his mistakes." Keith declared afterward that Barclay learnt the doctrine from him, and the writer produces proofs of this from Keith's writings. But the recent proofs of a common source in the writings of Schwenkfeldt, makes the enquiry less interesting.

* The Mennonites condemned all oaths, all war, all adornment in dress, and frivolity in conduct and conversation. They had times for silent prayer in their worship; they had no paid ministry; they taught that a university training alone did not fit a man for the ministry. They also set the fatal example of excluding from their membership those who married either unconverted persons, or Christians of other denominations. They had circulating Yearly Meetings like the early Friends.

But the followers of Caspar Schwenfeld were still more like Friends than were other Mennonites. The same authority says (p. 237):—"The teaching of Schwenkfeld and Fox was identical on three important points. First, on what is called the doctrine of the 'Inward Light, Life, Word, Seed, &c.' Secondly, on 'Immediate Revelation;' that is, that God and Christ in the person of the Holy Spirit, the Word of God, communicates with the human soul without the absolute necessity of the rites and ceremonies of the church, or of any outward means, acts or things, however important they may be. . . . Thirdly, that as a necessary consequence, no merely bodily act, such as partaking of the Lord's Supper or Baptism, can give the inward and spiritual reality and power of the Lord's 'body and blood,' or that of the spiritual 'washing of regeneration;' nor can the soul be maintained in spiritual union with him by bodily acts." Schwenkfeld and his followers therefore discarded baptism and the Lord's Supper.

have known their source. But it is evident that they were not received by him mechanically. They were assimilated, not swallowed; that which seemed to him chaff being separated from the wheat with intelligent appreciation, and such variations being introduced as his own experience and conscience indicated.

The Apology develops with systematic thoroughness, the doctrine of the "Seed" or "Light within." The "Light within" is given to every man in measure, whether he be born in Christian or heathen lands; and so has been given since the Creation. It manifests his sins with kindly severity. As it is attended to, it grows in clearness, more light is given until the whole soul is filled with light, and joy, and peace. At first, the "seed" lies all but dormant in the human soul, until its faint impulses are recognised, accepted and honoured. Then it grows in power, it subdues the corruptions of the flesh, it spreads its influence throughout the whole nature and the whole life. Its power is sufficient for every duty and for all righteousness. But the early Friends are not at all careful to maintain unity of idea and congruity of figure with regard to the terms "Light" and "Seed." They use them indiscriminately to describe the Divine In-dwelling in all its stages. They are the secret of man's capacity for salvation. Through the "Universal Light" all men may be led to a saving knowledge of God. It prepares the way for those "Immediate Revelations" of divine truth, which Barclay declares to have been the formal objects of faith in all ages. By these "Immediate Revelations" or discoveries of vital truth to the soul, and by these alone, every Christian becomes savingly acquainted with the things of God.

Like the Mennonites, the Quakers did not believe the Seed to have any vitality apart from the Spirit of God. Neither the early Friends nor any of their successors have ever believed in any natural power in man, by which he could savingly know God, or work out his soul's salvation. The seed or light was the gift of God; it was not the soul, as Barclay is careful to explain, but a "substance"* divinely given to every man, not naturally, but by grace. The seed was not separable from Christ, and when it was quickened, Christ was formed in the heart, and became the life of the soul.†

Another peculiar feature of the Quaker view of the Divine Indwelling is developed by Barclay in his chapter on Perfection. He has before claimed that justification is all as one with sanctification; he now explains that, in the view of Friends, regeneration implies the possibility of perfection in this life. He contends earnestly for a lofty view of the power of Christ in the believer. His proposition runs thus:—"Proposition VIII. In whom this pure and holy birth is fully brought forth, the body of death and sin comes to be crucified and removed, and their hearts united and subjected to the truth, so as not to obey any temptation or suggestion of the evil one, to be free from actual sinning and transgressing of the law of God, and in that respect perfect;

---

* Barclay uses the term in its scholastic sense as opposed to "attribute."

† The following extract will assist in correcting one mistaken idea of the "Light within." It is from a speech made in the Yearly Meeting of 1861, by my respected former tutor, Isaac Brown, whose solid learning and sound judgment have won him the greatest confidence amongst Friends. The notorious "Essays and reviews" were under discussion, and he said, "Some thought the work ought to be hailed by our Society, because of the views it advanced on the doctrine of the 'inward light.' He believed this idea was a misconception. The opinion of the Essayists appeared to coincide rather with those of the Hicksite body in America, than with those preached by George Fox and now held by our Society. It was not the 'inward light' (by which our early Friends clearly stated that they meant nothing else than the light of the Spirit of Christ) to which these writers referred us, but the 'enlightened reason.' He thought it was time for us to discontinue the use of this term 'the inward light,' as it had been grievously misinterpreted out of the Society, and was not found in Scripture."

Let me here say that any one may find the essentials of Quakerism without the Platonising doctrine of the "Seed," in J. J. Gurney's "Distinguishing Views and Practices of the Society of Friends."

yet doth this perfection still admit of a growth, and there remaineth always in some part a possibility of sinning, where the mind doth not most diligently attend unto the Lord."

From these and other teachings it has been inferred that the Friends did not believe in the earthly life and sacrificial death of our Lord; that they knew no Christ but the Christ within. This is a great mistake.* That they received and held these truths is a point easily proved, and Barclay distinctly affirms that they must be preached, or the believer will not become a complete Christian. But they argued that there might be Christian life without the knowledge of these truths. In their teachings the Christ within was prominent, and the death of Christ filled a less prominent position as the ground of God's mercy, the meritorious cause of the gift within.

But in perusing Barclay, the reader will of course remember the controversies out of which his works sprung, and will make allowance for the strain of debate. Points on which disputants are agreed will always be passed over slightly; points that have been overlooked or challenged will be emphasised, and dwelt on so largely as to seem out of proportion. But undoubtedly, when amongst the Friends of the next century these controversial works became the staple reading of an age of declining piety, the mischief done by this disproportion was great. Quakerism, contrary to the designs and aspirations of its early leaders, became almost synonymous with mysticism and quietism, and little better than theism. The objective facts of Christianity were neglected, and subjective experiences were everything. For instance in all the writings and Journal of John Woolman, admirable as they are in many respects, there is hardly a single statement of the atoning work of our Lord and Saviour.

---

* See the valuable letter, quoted p. 70.

Still the evangelical reader will find in Barclay much that he can enjoy and approve. His arguments for the necessity of the Holy Spirit's help in reading the Scriptures to profit, and in gaining a saving knowledge of Christian truth, are most excellent. So with many other points involving spiritual-mindedness. But the present writer heartily agrees with Joseph John Gurney, when, in the midst of the Beacon controversy he wrote, when Barclay's name was brought into special prominence, "I am, however, inclined to the opinion, that were we compelled to select a single writer in order to ascertain the religious principles of the Early Friends, we could scarcely do better than choose George Fox himself."* And this choice would be justified, not only by the clearness and fulness of Fox's expositions of Scripture truth, but by the healthy tone and practical power of those expositions. It is significant that Barclay and not Fox was the favourite writer of the Quietistic age of Quakerism.

For a long period Barclay was more than a standard writer amongst the Friends. His Apology had all the authority of a creed, and not to accept it would be sufficient to brand any Friend as unsound.† Nobler minds might feel that this was bondage utterly foreign to the spirit of the early Friends; yet a large number of Friends did not. But about the beginning of the present century, a change came over the Society. Religious and philanthropic works led some of its members to associate with evangelical churchmen and

---

* J. J. Gurney's Memoirs, vol. 2, p. 28.

† "The 'Apology' of Barclay was largely printed and distributed by the Society, and was accepted at the period of which we are treating [1833] (contrary to the principles of the ancient Society) as a *distinct creed*, which every person bearing the name of a 'Friend' ought to be prepared to accept in all its parts. * * * At this period it was deemed sufficient proof of I. Crewdson's doctrinal 'unsoundness,' to state that he objected to certain portions of the able theological treatise of Barclay." "R. Barclay's 'Inner Life of the Religious Societies of the Commonwealth,'" p. 573.

others. Controversies also arose, which at least compelled a systematic and critical study of the Bible. Broader sympathies and more enlightened study of the Scriptures undermined Barclay's influence. It was found that his exposition of Scripture texts was sometimes unsatisfactory. The Yearly Meeting ceased to print the Apology for gratuitous distribution, though not without strenuous protest from some, who clung to the old ways of presenting Quaker truth.

In the more recent literature of the Society, the doctrine of the Divine seed is scarcely to be found. But its essence is there. The illumination of the Holy Spirit, and the presence of Christ with his church are held by Friends with peculiar distinctness and force. The fact that all men have grace enough to accept the offer of salvation if they will, is stated as clearly now as it was by George Fox. Let there be but the zeal and the faith of George Fox, his urgency in dealing with men, his confidence in pleading with God, and Quakerism has yet a message that the world needs to hear, and that will win its olden triumphs, and bring its divine blessings to man.

www.ingramcontent.com/pod-product-compliance
Lightning Source LLC
Chambersburg PA
CBHW030336170426
43202CB00010B/1144